The President of Planet Earth

THE PRESIDENT
OF PLANET
EARTH

DAVID WHEATLEY

Wake Forest University Press
Winston–Salem, NC

THE PRESIDENT OF PLANET EARTH

Wake Forest University Press
Post Office Box 7333
Winston-Salem, NC 27109
WFUPRESS.WFU.EDU
WFUPRESS@WFU.EDU

First North American edition

ISBN 978-1-930630-83-3
Library of Congress Control Number 2017931443

Designed and typeset by Caron Andregg
SEACLIFFMM.COM

Publication of this book was generously supported by the Boyle Family Fund.

for my brothers, Philip, Gavin, and John

CONTENTS

A BEE-HIVE

Sitting under the crook of the eaves
in my black and yellow jumper
I turn ultraviolet blue
in the gaze of a honeybee
I watch enter the roof.

Like a postman's round, the sex
drags on all morning, its fine
filigree residue dispatched
journey by journey to our
asylum of honeycombed dark.

All round me masterpieces
of morbid secretions find their
invisible form, perfection raised
to the level of self-devouring,
a stomach digesting its body.

The bounty of innumerable
foxglove lips parted
slaveringly has brought us to this:
a jelly pleasure sea
I float on, hapless acolyte

of a queen I nourish and dread.
Am I so much as noticed, I wonder,
I and my furious labours? I feel
the jelly throb with her need for me, me
and those billions of others, my kind.

MAKING STRANGE

Ce navire est à nous et mon enfance n'a sa fin.

Introit: The 1901 Census

Farmer, farmer, railway clerk, scholar.
Read and write, read and write, not known.

Lifting the latch between two centuries
and calling each of his pigs by name,

a waistcoated hireling strikes up
the songs of his people lustily,

lazily, lingeringly,
a phonograph needle biting the wax.

Pillar-box patriarch, thumbs
in his fobs, prepares a time capsule

in family memory
of shoe leather, whiskers and bacon,

Victoria's head on the stamps
later refranked with a harp.

His pigeon fancier's scullery window
still opaquely beshitten

a century later, wipe
with scouring pad or old rag as you will,

that flurry of wings and droppings
ominously thick in the air:

hup there, ya lad ya, to hell owwadat!

I remember—no, not remember what does not end.

Already the warm dark is taking its leave of me.

I'm not going back.

Isn't he the image of her, the living image?

Borne from the city down one of two routes that divide at the Dodder and the Irish Sweepstake Building, the lottery of the high or the low road yielding the same small jackpot, home.

A cuddly toy on a grabber in Dawson's Amusements: hooked, hoisted and (wait for it) dropped.

There are other cuddly toys; there is no other town. Shudder go the floorboards as the ghost train rattles round its circuit, and again as the black and amber diesel dawdles past to Wexford, train upon train but only one destination for you—can we always live in Bray, Mam?—the pincer of Bray Head and the harbour's fingers holding the prize in place, never to be let go.

A cup of mashed-up bread and water, then someone closing his eyes and sticking his finger in it: Nelson's eye. The invisible past a glutinous pulp between your fingers, a long-dry socket suddenly moist again.

Across the sea came Mantan, the gap-toothed, crazed in the head, chanting impiety, jeered at and stoned.

Wicklow a slack-jawed skull on the map, chewing on Carlow, side-burned with hills, and the back of its head full of swans in the harbour and me.

Flick of the Town Hall wyvern's tail.

The babe-in-arms shrieks and demands to be lowered to play on the hexagon tiles on the hotel floor. All touches, connects, bites and locks together.

Do not touch me: I do not wish to be touched ('when you finish combing my hair I will have finished hating you').

Did you ever in your life hear the like of it!, says Mam.

Held upside while my hair is shampooed and rinsed in the kitchen sink, then righted again, and attempting to suckle the taps' two witchy-blue spouts.

Carved in the bridge over the river that took the traveller's daughter, a child's footprint: impotent against the tide, the blade slicing instead through yielding stone.

Pee-puddle spreading speculatively over the PE hall floor where I sit. Then dragged off to the boys' room by Auntie Brenda, soggily disgraced and unrepentant.

Sure you have my heart scalded!

Sinbad the ragdoll sailor, our narrator, voyages nightly below the pillow, surfs the hot water bottle's gurgling currents before resurfacing, breathless. Pyjama atolls lurk there, treacherous Dinky car reefs.

Darting from the car to the door you—I blurring into you—you beat on the glass and smash it. In case of emergency break glass. Knocking on glass today it is the scars of that other pane you feel on the ridge of your palm.

The door opens onto the dust of years and a space of light and empty waste (memory, that lumber room)—no, wait, onto rashers for tea and the telly on in the next room. Not rashers again!

Blue whoosh of a Superser rush-light flaring. Then out. Try again. As long as your finger stays on the button the flame will hold. As long as your finger—as long as—. Or cheat and stick a spoon in and go back to reading your *Dandy*.

Under and inside the table it is Moonbase Alpha, above and outside it is the 1940s, land of obligatory beetroot. Eat it all up now. Grandad is eating cabbage and fatty bacon in his waistcoat. That biro will have your eye out and no mistake.

Have you been over beyond to Derrylossary, he asks his brother. Would y'ever see about them slates from Calary. I have. I will. The whole shebang. The barometer needle has never been observed to move. You set it to Fair and the weather immediately improves.

Under the table is Moonbase Alpha but overhead is Skylab, doomed and seeking only your head in the crowd before it chooses its moment and—no, not yet. Your packet of Space Dust catches the meteor shower in its wake, bubbles popping all along your tongue where they crashland.

Twitch-buzz of a dying fly on the sitting room windowsill. An odour of death leaks from the Vapona hung from the ceiling, mixed with the Mr Sheen sharp in the airless room where Mammy is cleaning. Scour, wipe and spray, hide in your room while she.

Have you been at the chocolate again?, the airtight bag of it hoarded under the bed for Lent. Out with that Toblerone this minute!, the semi-chewed triangle spat into the kitchen sink to bob in the soapy dishwater.

The grasshopper tickles a song from its belly.

47! And this one? 53! And this one?, your school nurse questioner flipping the binder pages, its numbers hidden like camouflaged shells on the beach. Not colourblind then. And now for a quick root around in—*ahem*—that's a good lad—cough when I say.

We apologise for the interruption of this, the interruption of this—telly not working again—*hope to resume as soon as possible.* Mam, the button on the back you told me to press to stop *Treasure Island* while we went out didn't work, does that mean it's—*hope to resume...*—does that mean it's—*soon as possible*—broken—how do I make it... Ma-am! ... come back on?

Peanut butter and buttercup brown and yellow of the rusting chairlift on Bray Head. Next stop the cross, says Mammy, pretending. Make Daddy carry you anyway. Carry, carry me, Daddy!

A shout in the street: *hey you!* Who you? Say your name. *Is mise... is tusa...* I am... You are... grammatical-example-governing-use-of-the-copula is my name. *Dáithí. Is mise Dáithí.*

Track-suited women on their Sunday walks jerking their arms like skiers, the railings' orange orbs in bloom all the way down the prom. *Kennst du das land, wo die Zitronen blühn?* And the homeless man somewhere inside his layers stretched on the bench, eye to eye with the dog that licks his face while it pees.

Your parents' trysting ground, the International Hotel, the psychedelic browns, yellows, and oranges of its wallpaper and deep-shag carpets. Then up in flames with them all one evening, and you taken along to watch: the parallel life unled, your egg of unbeing broken and spilled. And the wrecking ball to finish it off, one more shell of infancy gutted, the memory of it left demolished and standing.

Three inferior copies of me, reproducing all my virtues and none of my flaws. Whose legs are they in the bed? Kicky Malicky. Number one has a little hair at the base of his thumb, just so, like mine, has always had. Asked about this years from now he will flatly deny it. Perhaps number two, number three, perhaps no one.

Reach for a nail-clippers and yank the hair out. The words 'Philip is cool' in spidery biro in the bottom drawer of a wardrobe, rediscovered during a house move in England thirty years later and left there.

Roar goes the snap dragon whose jaw you unhinge. Then sit hiding inside each of the hydrangea bushes one after the other, checking the time on the dandelion clock before coming out. Yummy says Philip, and puts a worm in his mouth. The worm wriggles its tail as it disappears in—no, out—no, into the ground—and roar goes the dragon again.

Hollow leathery thwack off the wall in Canon Crinion's handball alley. Old repeater, echo-chamber: strike it again.

There was the Triumph estate with the Mickey Mouse transfer on the bonnet that always made you carsick until we hung those strips from the bumper. Then there was the Alfa Romeo. Your brothers loved the Alfa. That would have been when your father had that beard of his hanging off his chin. Then there was the Mirafiori with a growl on it like you wouldn't believe from the clutch. Tell me, how does that old jalopy of yours keep going at all?

That's the way! A weakness for railway stations among the harmless mad. A worn old briefcase in one hand full of, what is it, pebbles or sand, he waves the Rosslare train on its way. Easy now: and she's off!

Terrible tragedy: derailment on the Hornby Dublin to Arklow diesel train; many killed, multiple injuries reported. The plastic engine left on its side while you go see if Mam brought Space Raiders back from Dunne's. But what's that—I *said* not mango and chutney!

CIE would like to apologise for the late arrival of the Connolly Train on platform one. This train is approximately forty years late.

Panini sticker stuck on my—stuck on my—can't get it—champions again this year then—can't get it off—finger.

The osprey feather in her trilby has fallen to earth from a genteeler pre-war decade. Ms Tyner of Ashford produces Aunt Maud's photograph album, smoothing it open on her rooftop snaps of 1916. In this one here you can see, to one side of the rubble, the elephant over Elvery's door, the sporting outfitter's. Of course they thought she was a sniper and took pot-shots back at her, which she didn't like one little bit. And what did we do then, Mam? Were we alive then?

By his broken, crossed legs, we recognise here a dead crusader, in the St Michan's crypt. Shake his hand, why don't you. Then—shouldn't have had that second Lucozade, should you—crossing your legs in the car all the way home—bags the jakes when we get there—it's 'toilet', say 'toilet'—I'm only burstin, so I am!

On his longest and most treacherous journey Sinbad will set out on a wee-wee tide beyond the known world of the bed sheets, where he will be captured and hung out to dry in Cuxhaven, Germany, home of grandfatherly walruses. Poor drowned Sinbad spoken of henceforth in whispers, needing only a tide of fellow seamen to wash him back home, but too soon for that, then re-emerged from under a pile of socks in Dad's suitcase. As he was saying earlier—

Run to the phone and ring when the mystery voice comes on the radio. Nanny says wireless. Engaged. Long wait for the 9 to rotate back when you ring. In the call box you press button A, or B, I forget. Which one was A and which one was—, I might ask now, on the phone to—I'll just hand you over to your...—, If I can just get a word in—, Which one was what, button what?, Did you know we have free calls now so I can...—, As I was SAYING—, Oh, forget it!

The papal contrails peter out fluffily over the playground, the rapier-tips of Master Lavin's index fingers jabbing Hail Marys skyward: what's that doing on Newsround? See what's on the other side. Cartoons, I hope. Young people of Ireland I..., something something, the LP Granny buys of his visit scratched to unplayable and repeating: Young people of, young people of...

From the burrawang tree falls Grug, one more teatime cartoon, his caveman hair a shock of fronds and vines. No, don't remember that one. You don't expect me to know them *all*, do you? From the pines in the FCA grounds you fall, time after time, through needled canopies, xylophoning cones, feeling the sap rise as you plunge. Bang, shout the bullet-less FCA men, parading lazily round the field, bang bang bang.

The number eight traced in fountain pen for your maths homework: figures of eight/infinity symbols traced on the ice where stove-pipe-hatted Netherlanders skate across the sitting room wall. Avercamp's *A Winter Scene*, all autumnal beech-leaf brown and greens, as of the mulch out the back where you've been gathering bonfire wood. Come goodwife, shall we disport ourselves in a decorous two-step on the ice, where the young master has come a cropper and brought down the minister with him? We shall and no mistake.

The low countries again: bowed, faceless figures; crows hurled skyward like smuts from the garden fire in Brueghel's *Hunters in the Snow*, through which you still trudge all these years later, head bowed, the dogs' legs sinking up their knees, the blue fingertips you will shortly warm at the bonfire flames.

The middle room in Nanny's we never sit in has a panel in the wall, awaiting a sudden peekaboo! through to the sitting room, to tea-cups and custard creams dropped in surprise. Isn't he the card. Bright as a button too! I'll say. Then off to see what Seánie is burning in his back garden today, black bituminous plumes twisting down the road all the way to The Punnet.

Salubrious waft of Mr Lynch the piano tuner's pipe smoke and a jabbing thumb on an upright Bechstein's middle C. Abrupt report of a tuning fork smacked on the sideboard, then stood to vibrate at concert pitch C. *Ker-thwonk!* Strike that note again. Something wrong there, says Sinbad. That's some dose, says Mam. Then when it's fixed, All tickety boo, says

Dad. Open the piano lid when Mr Lynch departs and make fairy music, plucked harmonics, on the strings, then close the coffin lid over them, sealing them in, in the dark.

Well in the merry month of May, sings Dad in the Tara Towers Hotel when in comes a billy-goat man, all primary colours like the test card—Luke Kelly—knocks back a—what's that called Dad, that's not a pint—gin and tonic and leaves—Hoor's drink!, shouting as he goes—is that a rude word?

Servants of St Bridget, the oystercatchers lined up on Booterstown Strand. A Bridget's cross on the RTE test card, not the girl with the clown and the blackboard. Noughts and crosses it is then. No wait, I *meant* to put the x in the middle: start again. Look Mam, Oxo, just like the cube! Then Rubik's cube. One side done. Peel off the stickers, all primary colours and cheat. Look, Mam, look!

Lancelot lopes from the Kilruddery undergrowth, swinging a claymore towards the passing Greystones bus. Serpent's breath, charm of life and death. *And, cut!* Something to talk about in the playground. I'm King Arthur then, no *I'm* King Arthur, settled amidst much shoving. *The Excalibur Drive brings you through some of the most spectacular and varied landscape in County Wicklow.* The land has been struck with famine and sickness, says Percy. Soup and sandwiches in the Roundwood Inn?, asks Dad.

Redcoats blow their horns from the walls and pitch the bomb-balls down, guardians of the reservoir. The obedience of the citizenry makes for the city's delight. And down the steep grass banks you go, shrieking. Give us a dhrink o' wather. Pretend to flick one of John's jellybeans into the lake and tell him it will come out the tap when we get home. Eat jellybean and produce another from your pocket at home. *But my one was blue!*

Mrkgnao, shrieks a catless childhood, a solitary feline erupting, disturbed, from under your bed one evening and off down the stairs.

The purple lady in Mam's embroidery, wide-skirted among flowers, purple flowers. The lavender field by the dual carriageway in Kilmac as we drive past: get a good whiff of that. The purple lady. Clip-on earrings' purple flowers. More needlework at the kitchen table: thread me that needle there with your sharp eyes. Come here to me now till I—

If the crab on the beach could only try to walk sideways, he would go straight.

The Fassaroe pit is a sandy wound in the earth, gouged deeper and thinner while you tricycle round Dad's workshed, lorry-drivers coming and going. For 'lorry' read 'lurry', a stricken Foden on its side, Uncle David posing for a snap beside it. To grit sand add shingle, ballast and hardcore and lay as required.

The trail of footsteps you leave in the sand leading by a short detour to a tar bed steaming all the way up Quinsboro Road, and—watch this Gav—the footsteps you will leave in that too. Or—kindly stop that now, young man—words to that effect—maybe the next time.

Up the hill drifts the shrill peep-peep from the station again. The black and amber caterpillar hugging the Headland has yet to graduate to butterfly and may never, following the arc of the cove where the signal box winks and the flat stones bask in the greeny-blue shallows.

Brunel's ghost tunnel, to be run down screaming, trailing a plastic bag with your togs full of sand as you go. His live tunnels, ditto. (Better again on slow trains home a window lowered, then clinging on, kicking the door from under you, and whoosh! the wait for it to snap back into place.)

The train trip from Bray to Greystones a series of empty stages—tunnel, cove, tunnel, cove—between the tracks and the sea, or framing a ferry, a freighter, rows of cormorants unmoved in the stalls, where the signal shelter sits windowless but occupied, *casa dei doganieri*, its line of chimney smoke pulled out to sea where the fulmars' foul mouths scream and spit.

The Harbour Bar to the Brandy Hole, my life by water—

Cuprous old penny placed on the tracks as the diesel passes, recovered afterwards slightly flattened but none the worse for that. Then pocketed for the penny falls in the Star Amusements, the leaping salmon on my last ten-pence piece saved for the Space Invaders. The train door snaps back, the penny drops, and well before teatime invaders have conquered the earth.

Its green patina scraped off the old penny, dog shit picked from my runners with a stick in the garden *(have you checked the other one too?)*. Cover a sheet in crayons for Master Cronin, cover the colours in black then remove with the back of a spoon to reveal unsuspected stick-men below, lurking henceforth in every darkness, fiery-orange and red homunculi dancing in the fire after tea.

Tá daidí ag obair, tá mamaí sa chistin. But Mammy is working and Daddy is in the kitchen, chopping the mince, conjugating gender roles and irregular verbs. The rude words not in the dictionary. Action Man is smooth down there, when you check. Dolls you can't speak for. Cough now, the nurse says again, the cheek of it: I have balls! I have two balls!

He does be liking his tea at five, amn't I after telling you. Frequentatives of corned beef and mash, dialectal isobars visible on the weather forecast map at the end of the news. But first—plate balanced on your knees while you eat—time for *Ivor the Engine.*

Wrapped in paper inside the colcannon, I mean curly kale, a slight obstruction: tuppence, the tooth fairy on the instalment plan.

C — E — G — C — G — E — C. G — B — D — G — D — B — G. D — F — something wrong there. Sharp, sharp! Half-hour's practice before school in the morning, the neighbours loving it, *2000 AD* up on the stand while you do the arpeggios then falling into your lap.

Then during the war Bridie went to London, says Dad back from a funeral—went to London, said the priest, and met Dan Dare. Can you imagine it, Dan Dare. The Mekon leans forward on his flying dish (puny spaceman, what can you do against my unlimited power) before dismissing the earthling and levitating off about his business, the extermination of all human life, then a bike-ride down the stream with David and David and Alan and Maurice and Dáire.

Uncle Ted, wheezing elephant seal of a man dressed in burgundy and mustard, pulls up in his Wolseley, walnut-effect dash and radiator badge fresh from a Sunday waxing. In driving gloves, too. He bears a Christmas offering of mouldy biscuits, nibbled, discarded. Glass of sherry? Only the one, thanks, the smell of damp corduroy warming in front of the fire, sickly, old-mannish. Or maybe another, he reconsiders, while I'm here.

Eyes level with the counter of his featureless shop, Mr Delimata stares through the window at his trim Wartburg outside, facets of distant Polish beginnings visible through his jeweller's eyepiece. The old country, the new country. The other country. Uncle J dead in Zürich, cousin L over in England. On his wife's side, this would be. What's for Christmas dinner? Then a Chopin mazurka or two on the piano and a walk round the harbour, knots of the overfed bored still wearing the hats from their crackers and offering Christmas cake to the swans.

Lesser-known Irish saints: Banbhan, Colman, Maolruadhan. The Aer Lingus fleet, the Presentation Brothers' house. The unknown Brother. Next stop Cahirciveen!, his shout from the wardrobe. Next stop the science lab sin-bin. In there with you now, snaps Brother Justin, then sits on the lid, bad cess to you anyway. The young folks at home, no dignity left. Acupuncture pins in Brother Wolfe's ear, the flutter of his leather strap tongue-lashing the air. If I have to bate it into you, so help me God—

Talc, gypsum, calcite, fluorite. Learn about rocks and minerals organised by hardness, streak, lustre, cleavage, fracture, specific gravity, narrates Sinbad. Apatite, triphyllite, feldspar. Here we observe hitherto unnoticed radiating fanlike impressions in the Cambrian rocks on Bray Head. Quartz, beryl, topaz, corundum, grey wax—sorry, greywackes. Silurian era batholiths seething and spitting in the Iapetus Ocean, with what is Bray now somewhere south of the equator.

Notice too the micaceous schists, the more recent scratches not perhaps the work of geological forces. *Ger Loves Niamh. Shankill Geebags.* Splash, goes Bray arriving from the south seas with an almighty bang. The granite magma that underlies you too, visible and throbbing each time you fall off your bike.

First Confirmion, I mean Confirmunion, a badly knotted tie and odours of chrism and incense; body of something stuck in the roof of your mouth. More Space Dust handy for that. Still, worth a digital watch. A clutch of balloons escapes at the end and bump against the church ceiling like the levitating Joseph of Cupertino, making a holy show of himself at mass again. You work the wafer free and it bobs straight back up whence it came.

Your front teeth complete a slow approach, touch and cross. The crumbs of decades will collect there, collect there still. Drunken molars buckling this way and that, tiny Judases wanting their thirty pieces of silver. Fabled crustacean, your brace lurks in its glass of water at night, with a nasty bite on it for the unwary: ouch!

That was our house where those officers were shot in their beds, Ms Tyner continues. My father was sure that but for the door he put in at the side, the shootings would never have happened, and felt very guilty. I remember meeting Michael Collins, Mr Ó Broin tells Dad, he gave me a watch. Pressed it very firmly into my hand. An upright coffin of a grandfather clock strikes and an antique kettle comes to the boil in the kitchen. Then later a mechanical coffee pot drives onto the pitch in Croke Park, Bray, and opens fire on the crowd, Neil Jordan directing. Black and Tans out, Brits out of the Prince of Wales Terrace, the Carlisle Grounds now!—*And, cut!*

Finish your beetroot, there's a good man, eat it all up! Granny's cheeks the same ruddied purple by now, you flinching from the vitamin flush and the kiss goodbye afterwards, who don't know you're born, but all too born to the family drive and Sunday afternoon visit, eyes down and picking moodily at the mince.

Over the high wall by the house goes a schoolbag slung and a trespasser-dawdler fearing the slavering dogs only for hastening him on his way. Over the wall goes a football now spiked in gehennas of brambles, offside anyway, a low *pfft* of relief escaping its bladder.

'Zebedee he / Did climb a tree / Our Lord to see...', no, something wrong there, a jack-in-the-box impostor spring-loaded into my RK copy to Brother Horgan's disgust. Fail!

When objects collide or explode in space they do so in silence.

Skylab falls.

Ireland comes unstuck and moves to the centre of the map, Christian Brothers following the arrows and scattering round the globe, Ireland the navel, umbilically linked to the little black babies. One fruity stray trouser salute during singing and Brother Horgan cancels our trip to the mushroom farm. A fountain pen is impounded, and revenge taken on a box of chocolates, his Christmas offering: the top layer raided, the rattling remainder handed over with not so much as a blush.

Master Barry's quick hand traces, conceals a digit on the blackboard. What was it? Quicker than the wrong answer the chalk propelled through the air, its contact with you smarting still.

A seagull takes aim and deposits its load of guano smack on Brother Forde's dome in the playground one morning: remembered or imagined, imagined-remembered?

Stay there till we put out the rubbish, I said. Brother Justin again. Yet when you emerge it is Brother Justin and all his kind who have departed.

Before the game begins each player creates his or her player character. Sorry, who am I again?, you ask the role-playing years. Can I fly? How do I fly? *Trivial actions are usually automatically successful.* Kick Gav in the— ouch, stop it. No wait, I'm dead. *It is often possible for a dead character to be resurrected through magic.*

These quartzite flecks in the path, the hills baring their long bones under the gorse where they stretch their haunch by the sea. The gaudy Marian cross on the summit, a sugary cake-top cairn. The giants who bestrode these mountains walked from summit to summit. Djouce's roches moutonnées scooped by the wind, a heart-shaped corrie above the cloudline, a heart shape traced in your coffee in the overpriced gift shop below.

And County Wexford for a bit of sun in the summer and strawberries on the way in Enniscorthy. A wobbling caravan, brown with inspissated residue of summers past.

Sinbad looking out to sea at the pepper-pot Kish: short stroke, short stroke, long stroke. On a good day you can see Wales from the Head, on a better day see Bray Head disappearing from the car-ferry deck, the parallax view. Circuits of the lounge and trying the video games for stray ten pees; shudder from under your feet of the huge lorries, nose to tail, waking up in the hold. Then some Toby jugs in a window in Holyhead, a trip to Woolworth's and home.

Starting from Sally Gap where X marks the spot turn left for Luggala's punch bowl, right for Poulaphouca's drowned villages, and straight on for further, deeper in, the glacial valleys brushing the mountains aside like your mother's fingers run effortlessly through her hair.

Striking out over the fields behind Lough Dan and lost. Wait, Dad says, it's this way—

The *Record Breakers* man plays albums by feeling the grooves and singing the tunes. Get thumbprints all over yours and—no, doesn't work. Then try them backwards and devil this, devil that, you've been led to believe— no, doesn't work either. Try 'Rockin All Over the World': drag the needle backwards and—can't hear anything—the needle jumping out of your hand like a boom down the harbour. And I like it, I like it, I—must be scratched—gets a bit boring. The needle bored too, falling asleep on its pillow of fluff at the end, firing off rhythmical snores like Trigger the dog, I mean Mitch.

Unpeel their sellotape and release the plastic Spitfires stuck to the cover of *Warlord* and *Victor*, owl-pellets of someone else's war: their line grounded decades later in the lifesize model outside an abandoned Airfix factory in Hull, East Yorkshire, opposite the smelting furnace, graffitoed *I love you Mam.*

Kaleidoscopic amoebas, ten feet tall, nuzzle, merge and part on the Ormonde Cinema screen before the main feature, *Sinbad the Sailor* in Technicolor. Up with this sort of thing! Images that yet fresh homages beget, pools of sick behind the love-seats. And during the intermission too, choc-ices all round.

A sticky darkness, warm smells and the battle for the arm-rest: mine. King Kong tumbles off the Empire State Building and through the screen, his death-agonies surviving the walk to the car and beyond: take that, fighter plane/brother!, all the way home. Cut it out there in the back: none of that codology now!

Swinging from human hand to hand in Nanny's back garden—my turn, no *mine*—rubber King Kong stretches and snaps, tumbling into the long grass and there still, for all you know, waiting his chance to escape.

Blind amoebas swim in the tray in Mr Owens' dark room, from your go on the antique box camera one Sunday. Low tide's fugitive meniscus outside the Harbour Bar washing over the simple box camera lens: snap. Sheepskin coat, woolly hat, and the tail-end of Mam's Jackie Onassis hair-do—Jackie who?—snap. A sticker marked 'free' on the spoils: some puddle of black and white mess, events that occurred less than once hereby memorialized.

Focus cannot be adjusted, then or now. Must have been when Dad distracted me with his. Look awry and see right. The purpose of the stop bath is to halt development. That smell of vinegar in the air. Transfer into the album, then keep in the press under the wooden elephant, I mean giraffe, and show to Auntie June. Then Dad buys the Nikon and colour is born: the brightness drains from your jumper, your bike and into packets of photographs you will never take out or show anyone.

Family memory as geology, local history as shifting rock formations. George Plant, genial assassin, stalks the hills: Grandad chugging around in the Citroën taxi while Quislings in waiting parachute over the heather by night, the rollrock highroad roaring down over the Featherbed Mountain. Nanny buried yards from the illegal organisation's founder, the colour party's sunglasses throwing the October sunlight back in my face.

You wouldn't be mixing with that crowd, the Garda at the door asking Mam, following us back from the graveyard. The good old boys!, snorts Dad, disgusted, drinkin' whisky and rye. Some day the mountain might get 'em but the law never will—no, wait, wrong song. Them Duke boys again, up to no good, snorts Boss Hogg, disgusted.

Curlews, what does a man have to do to find a curlew round here anymore. Striding on into cloud on the Lug, hours from the top: it's just over there, Dad announces.

The nest she sat in, of vodka bottles and Coke cans, the furnace-faced woman outside the library shouting at passers-by. Don't catch her eye. And then to the post office to draw her mother's pension and mind it for her, her mother's baffled face in the window at home looking out over the fields and the new factory. That time she chopped down the tree in the neighbour's garden, that time she fell under the Dart—just hang up when she calls, over and over and over.

Mick the Book: librarian as metaphor, synecdoche rather, the Sinbad, Ulysses rather, of the issue desk. Only let Gaybo have one of his radio quizzes and there's no end to it, says Mam, working in the library now. Sample answers: French Guiana, the Eucharistic Congress, *Darby O'Gill and the Little People.* Raised-arm salute across the street, as of a Clare hurler plucking a *sliotar* out of the air. To strive, to seek, to find ('You might like this')—copy of *Waiting for Godot.* They wait and he never turns up—how mad is that!

Bones as geology on fast-forward. Off snaps a part of your kneecap and forms a Little Sugarloaf above your right shin. Try kneeling at mass with an Osgood-Schlatter. Good excuse not to go then. Complete resolution may occur at skeletal maturity, explains Dr Liston, or may never. How are those spots of yours, he continues, tapping your knee. *Ubi pus, ibi vacuit.*

A great-grandfather's dates mirror Robert Frost's: 1874–1963. A road not taken, New Hampshire to Knocknaguilkey. A big roaring man with a great big red beard, says Sinbad.

Test Wheatley, the Arklow cricketer, John Wheatley, the Glasgow MP. The Wheatley murder. Tom Wheatley, hanged for a yeoman in '98. David Wheatley, TV producer. Look, look, it's your namesa– Do we *have* to watch this, Dad?

Any day now, Skylab—wait for it wait for it—

A dayglo foetus huge on a placard, blue-veined sightless eyes beady and throbbing, like a prawn from the Jasmine House on the Main Street. None for me thanks, ringing for a takeaway, just spring rolls and noodles.

Against the trunk of our tree house a stream of liquid relief, seeping into the mulch and feeding the beanstalk we climb to peer over the canopy into the German's estate.

Oystercatchers pick at the bladderwrack in the crook of the promenade's arm by the Bray Head Hotel, Mam's curling tongs threading her hair. Oh, but they pinch and burn! The sea anemones of her green clip-on earrings. Oh, but they pinch too!

The coalman tramps down the hall to the bunker behind the bathroom in Nanny's, the dust from the coal settling over the slick in the dark, the salt in the kitchen settling over the bangers and mash. Did he take his boots off. Did coalmen take their boots off then. No. Memory's heavy tread not taking its boots off, but tramping, tramping, tramping.

The hotel barmaid wipes a pint glass, removes her glass eye, wipes it down too, and back in it goes.

Who's for an auld singalong, Mam pipes up on the drive home one Sunday. A common driver's response to such musical moments being to drum one's fingers lightly on the wheel.

Slowly round their plastic maze the mercury droplets swim. Slowly inside my mouth my buckling teeth cross another micro-millimetre. Dr Flood will see you now. Garden tomtits perch and invert on the feeder in ones and twos. Dr Flood inserts the dental wedge and down you bite, hard, on the putty, breathing heavily, adenoidally, while it sets, admiring the watercolours on the surgery wall of the garden tomtits swooping for nuts.

Edie, the redcaps are back, Dr Flood calls through the partition, Edie, that cat's still around. The mould of my jawline awaits me on my next visit, ready to scuttle from Dr Flood's hand and seek out the cave of my mouth. Say Ah. Wider. My glottis a-quiver, King Crimson red. Wisdom teeth impacted and the X-rays to prove it, a ziggurat of molars, incisors, make sense of their crazy-paving who may. In goes the brace, my newest snapping crustacean, locking on tight.

Insuperable urge—*Health and Efficiency,* on the top shelf—of the large-breasted naked to cycle and play table-tennis. Clenching and unclenching the balls of your feet on the spot, a new-found fascination with the cover of *Angler's Monthly.*

The pursuit of knowledge as a series of forty-minute plays; the five-year avoidance of a falling rugby ball, any falling rugby ball. Raise your pseudopod to speak. Chivalry and honour, gentlemen. Ah lads, ah lads! Boy, come here boy, come over here boy! Mr Dingle, face to the blackboard and butting it gently: To follow knowledge like a sinking something beyond the utmost reach of something something.

———

Frantic blackboard epics in Irish class: wayfarers in a typhoon, scrambling eastwards then starting again from the left and overtaking themselves. Repeat after Mr Ó Gráinne: *fadhb na ndrugaí, fadhb na dífhostaíochta*, 'the problem of drugs, the problem of unemployment'—Sir, will that be coming up on the paper—repeat after me—shedding foul papers and unmarked scripts as he tears off with the bell. Sir, can I—pseudopod!— but Sir, can I—I *said* pseudopod! Then slope off down the beach with Finbarr and Conor and Oisín and Keith.

Mornings Dad hogs the mirror, poking a toothpick at the remains of his breakfast. Film of plaque and scum coating your rarely-used smile. Have you tried floss, booms over his shoulder. But there is no exit from the mercury labyrinth, your mouth full of supernumerary molars, yellowing, crumbling, the putty still full of your bite marks.

A slide, or slither, as though along the deck of a sloping boat, to the edge of the holiday photos. Sulky little bastard that you are. Then under the rim of a beret, then off the edge entirely, not to return.

Upward-creeping line of suburban sprawl on Little Sugarloaf's slopes, Lego bricks stacked on an unsuspecting cat asleep by the fire.

Run over and pick up your Dad, would you, asks Mam from the sofa. To Sallynoggin on your provisional licence, to wait in the chug of cars by the gates until a known shape steps from the fog and hands you a Listerine bottle. Good for the breath, he explains. Just in time for the headlines at ten then. People will always need Listerine. No, not 2FM, they don't do the scores—no need to be sulky—that needs third gear! *Good evening, listeners. Quite the most natural tenor voice I ever heard, captured here on 78—* what is this stuff—*United nil, Liverp–* — What's that on your cheek, have you been picking your—I told you, it's *nothing*.

Slithery-lathery-leathery-slathery. And back it goes. Hm, so that's how it works. No you can't come in—where's the lock on that bathroom door—I *said* I'm having a bath.

Late down to breakfast this morning. The dead arose and appeared to many, says Mam.

But the quincunx of heaven runs low.

To the Leaving Cert Irish oral examiner, announce: 'I inherit from my father my terrible teeth, from my mother my backache, and claim as my own my abominable temper. I boast on my mother's side direct descent from Patrick Sarsfield, and on my father's collateral ancestry with Lester Piggott. I was always such a well-behaved boy, shining at spelling. "Antidisestablishmentarianism." I stood on the grassy ridge (a sleeping giant) in Merrion Park across the way from the hospital, willing on my brother's arrival and repeating the performance three, five years later; they have never ceased to be grateful.'

'At the top of the hill was the new supermarket, at the bottom the school where we prayed for the cameras during the papal visit. Come September, we kissed goodbye to our girlfriends at the last summer project disco, then saw them again the following year. Disconsolately we stood in the GAA field on our school trip to Wexford, bearded by a resident *camán*-wielding savage. Apparently our being from Wicklow qualified us as "Jackeens": not a nice thing to be, in that part of the world. The big thick ignorant oaf.' Thank you, that will be all.

Back from the pool—the condemned, closed, built-over pool—back from the pool these years, the hard-to-shake residue of chloroform, sorry, chlorine on your fingers.

Kish to Poolbeg to Howth, the Dublin bay flasher still at it, Sinbad stuck in the mud at low tide. Symbol of something or other, all this time. Or not. Sad mere stony thereness symbolizing nothing at all.

Spell out in Braille the message constellations of acne have spelled on your cheeks, a reservoir of greasy disaffection full to overflowing. What are you doing in there, shouts John hammering on bathroom door. No, not that. Splatsplash daily refreshing the mirror's disgust at your face. The rage of Caliban at, something something. Ariel may have the rest of your teens off. This latest spot on your chin has something important to tell us. Quick, to the bathroom: out with it, out with it!

Perched of a summer morning in the tree-house, dream of scaling the tower on the mysterious German's land by the stream. Then as a teenager your one desire to play the pipes like Johnny Doran. Pass Rathnew with its Wimpy bar and plaster Madonna, where rests Doran, king of the travelling pipers, one chanter's toss from the Wicklow bus and the radio tuned to country'n'Irish.

Among the most important effects on the pipes the contrast between C natural and C sharp, as witness in so many piping tunes, Doran's 'Rakish Paddy' for one. Consider how differently he does it on the two recordings of that track, working the regulators each time like a pack of hounds on the chanter's trail.

Some pipers play open, some closed. Doran played open. You prefer closed, but prefer Doran's open to any good reasons why you might prefer closed. Hoist that chanter off the knee for those low Ds and Es, let the fox bark all it wants!

Pipeless today, look up as the bus passes the cemetery and wonder where you have buried your music. Sometimes he plays C natural, sometimes C sharp. Perched of a summer morning in the tree-house dream of scaling the tower on the mysterious German's land by the stream. Then as a teenager your one desire to play the pipes like Johnny Doran.

Checking your watch, you find it melting onto the cover of an old Penguin. *The Triangular Hour. Nausea.* Nausea. Your childhood large-print *Ivanhoe* is taken ill, is discreetly sick in the corner.

'Entering Milan on horseback in 1819...' Entering the gates of the college in your seventeenth year, you have instinctively acquired the words 'farouche', 'braggadocio', 'sprezzatura' and 'popinjay'.

'No sooner did the carbon dioxide of the novelty sweet touch my palate', the amusements giving way to summer reading now, 'than a shiver ran through me and I stopped, intent upon the extraordinary thing that was happening to me. Namely—' no, not yet, but coming, coming.

Today I would weigh your absence, childhood, in chattered stone, in pebbles clattering up Bray beach, in the Motte stone's terminal weight. Commuter traffic as drug mainlined through new arteries, a motorway slashed through a childhood picnic site, that day out with a great-aunt in a headband, fussing and excitable. A cancelled tram slides into the station. The settling residue of unbuilt developments past, the nettle-choked lanes by Barrington's Tower—Foley's Folly—a lone dog barking behind a security fence.

New road come out of nowhere on a trip home, depositing you behind the industrial park, furious in your borrowed car. Can't you turn that back windscreen wiper off? — I've tried, I—! —Just turn off and restart! Ways of the world, have we not followed you: knowingly, unknowingly, the still there, the gone.

The quiet of before the big money years and the quiet of after, the commotion in between missed: I was not here. A weariness of ghosts, a weariness of obsolescence eked out, your picked-over past, clean and unforgiving now as a herring bone stuck in the throat.

Decked out in drayhorses, Hiaces, stereos, mobile phones, all in marble and laid on a shark's-tooth bed of green-glass pebbling, the travellers' graves show signs of recent attention. Here are rosary beads draped from a headstone, plastic-wrapped flowers, offerings for the thirsty earth, drunk and undrunk, and a replica Liverpool shirt; someone's grief that will have left its imprint on trousers or knees where the grass is disturbed and the soil shows, soft and accommodating, on which we might kneel, we too, to consider the dead.

The hill-tops are ferry chimneys sailing past: glimpsed through a ferry window Bray Head becomes Little becomes Big Sugarloaf becomes, wait a minute, Bennachie. Where? Something wrong there says—are you still here?—says Sinbad.

Man, fish, barnacle goose. Dad stops the car on Featherbed Mountain, sees an armchair on the hillside, sits and poses for a photo. Anywhere round here for a—shouldn't have had that second coffee. A thin trickle covers the pebble-dashing behind the memorial (I once knew to what) then loses itself in the peat. Then back down past the war cemetery, down—what kind of time do you call this, says Mam—towards the lights of old.

Or back for Christmas: the meet-ups for drinks, the last place on the edge of the sofa after dinner, a Stephen's day stravaig on the prom. And then the turn-off for Kilmac or Newtown hallucinated near a junction on the M62, the taste of nanny's rashers rising unbidden up in a service station breakfast somewhere between Leeds.

Have you all your accoutrements, Dad asks as you're leaving, Mam adjusting your collar before you've finished putting your jacket on.

A pebble picked up on Bray beach and carried for years, turned over lovingly—carried and carried—lost.

A song of home rehearsed and rehearsed—to be sung on your journey—
to be sung when you get there—forgotten.

Wait, says Mam as you stomp down the hall, you—(applies wet finger
to cheek).

Losing our path and thrashing through gorse on the way down the Lug:
wait, says Dad, I know a way—

ON THE DEATH OF A POET

composed during the last illness of Eochaidh Ó hEodhasa

Poetry is touched by decline:
how can we come to her aid?
She is sure all hope is gone
in her poorly state.

Consider poetry's plight,
fit only for the sickbed
as word of Eochaidh's death is brought
to her who was his bride.

It is hard to witness the honour
once hers turn to scorn:
woeful indignity drawing near,
the cloud of abasement come down.

To Eochaidh above all men she gave
the flower in its prime
of her artistry and love;
and all to nourish him.

The hidden ore of his poet's craft
burned with a gemlike flame
lighting up the art he left;
much died with his name.

Well he knew the schoolmen's work,
who sat among the wise;
poet of the golden cloak,
a great lament shall be his.

He stumbled on the hazel of knowledge
in its secret grove,
and left its branches hung with flesh,
stripping the nutshells off.

Out of words both dark and subtle
the poet makes his art

with perfect ease, and in recital
omits no part.

It is no small help to his work
to add the gold relief
of learning to his every word:
such is the way of the beehive.

Bees all over brim their hoard
with the juice they collect
from the oozings of a milky gourd
or a flower unpacked.

They are examples to the bard
whose craft none can match;
no flower or fruit, soft or hard,
escapes his search.

It is he resolves the doubts
of those already skilled;
he who settles all debates,
he to whom all yield.

Who has not been touched by sorrow
at the master's loss of life?
This disease goes to the marrow
and pierces like a spike.

Like a cow parted from her calf,
my wits are overthrown;
I make melody from my grief,
who now am orphaned;

and poetry is a widow unless
Maoilseachlainn's son returns;
no-one can make good her loss
but the man she mourns.

      (from the Irish)

IN GLENMALURE

Crimson our halberds from the gore of the Saxons!
The firebrand soon secured and our sword arms aching.
Affliction our foes' part and Fiach McHugh O'Byrne
honoured at the pig feast by rivers of mead;
shrill from the dark high glen the bleating of sheep
while in and out of the mist floats Lugnaquilla.

The Castle styles Michael Dwyer a common killer
and, be it hereby known, will spare no expense
in his apprehension. Caught, this felon will ship
to New South Wales there to lament, ochone,
at his leisure his exile from old Wicklow amid
Fenians who barely 'scaped hanging like Billy Byrne.

An old man I passed by the monument to the O'Byrne
deep in the glen, his face a sunburnt colour,
had about him so melancholy a mood
I felt the spirit of that mountainous expanse
convert us, strangers, into almost kin
in that quiet corner where a man could sleep.

Early one morning a fair maid I met on the slope
of Ballinacor, her dark eyes heavy with brine
from weeping for her dear one unjustly taken,
the blackbird of sweet Avondale who would call her
his *leannán*, his darling from the tree-top in accents
so soft that for that want of them she was unmade.

Farmyard cottages ready to view, all mod
cons, no chain. Give the recession the slip
where money doesn't swear, it talks sense.
Take in the pine woods' late autumnal auburn
round picture-postcard-pretty Lugnaquilla
between the waterfall and perennial bracken.

Driving down into Glenmalure, not speaking,
the road flooded, the wheels spinning in mud:
O Fiach McHugh! Waiting for the shower to clear,
getting out, walking, feeling the damp seep

through my boots down the accursed boreen
where I revved and tried in vain to turn on a sixpence.

And crueller than all weather loom again
those peaks on the line of the sky that still drive mad
the woebegone sheep astray where the gorse fires burn.

all air all air all air all air all air all air all air all air all air all air all
all air all air all air all air all air all air all air all air all air all air all
all air all air all air all air all air all air all air all air all air all air all
all air all air all air all air all air *iolar* all air all air all air all air all
all air all air all air all air all air all air all air all air all air all air all
all air all air all air all air all air all air all air all air all air all air all
all air all air all air all air all air all air all air all air all air all air all
all air all air all air all air all air all air all air all air all air all air all
all air all air all air all air all air all air all air all air all air all air all
all air all air all air all air all air all air all air all air all air all air all
all air all air all air all air all air all air all air all air all air all air all
all air all air all air all air all air all air all air all air all air all air all
all air **doiléir** all air all air all air all air all air all air all air **soiléir** all air
all air **douleur** air all air all air all air all air all air all air all **solar** air all
all air **dealer** all air all air all air all air all air all air all **sailor** air all
ouler ouler ouler ouler ouler ouler ouler ouler ouler ouler ouler ouler
ouler ouler ouler ouler ouler ouler ouler ouler ouler ouler ouler ouler
ouler ouler ouler ouler ouler ouler ouler ouler ouler ouler ouler ouler
ouler ouler ouler ouler ouler ouler ouler ouler ouler ouler ouler ouler
ouler ouler ouler ouler ouler ouler ouler ouler ouler ouler ouler ouler
ouler ouler ouler ouler ouler ouler ouler ouler ouler ouler ouler ouler
ouler ouler ouler ouler ouler ouler ouler ouler ouler ouler ouler ouler
ouler ouler ouler ouler ouler ouler ouler ouler ouler ouler ouler ouler
ouler ouler ouler ouler ouler ouler ouler ouler ouler ouler ouler ouler
ouler ouler ouler ouler ouler ouler ouler ouler ouler ouler ouler ouler
ouler ouler ouler ouler ouler ouler *iolar* ouler ouler ouler ouler ouler
ouler ouler ouler ouler ouler ouler ouler ouler ouler ouler ouler ouler
ouler ouler ouler ouler ouler ouler ouler ouler ouler ouler ouler ouler
ouler ouler ouler ouler ouler ouler ouler ouler ouler ouler ouler ouler
ouler ouler ouler ouler ouler ouler ouler ouler ouler ouler ouler ouler

TABLE-TALK OF JOHN JOLY, FTCD, ON THE GEOLOGICAL UNIFICATION OF IRELAND

'The subduction of Laurentia by Avalonia':
a geological allegory—the nymphs among the stones—
or Aesop's fable for our Young Earth brethren.

Archbishop Ussher and his creationism, how are you—
sophistry, sir, the fossils placed ready-made
in the earth the better to test our faith!

I make but a poor iconoclast, chipping away with
a pocket hammer on the storm beach of the Word,
but in the decay sequence of uranium atoms

I find an Ireland radioactive with promise
and threat: a quaking sod, a clock whose counting
down to zero no clockmaker set. In the name

of the god of deep time and Ireland's short
tradition of nationhood I annotate dark
visions of her unification half a billion years since

for the *Proceedings of the Royal Irish Academy,* and not
a Kaiser's rifle or teapot armoured car in sight.
Laid down amid impossible magma plumes

and ramparts of volcanic isles the Paleozoic schists
and quartzite of Bray Head, the Himalayan
igneous basalts of Connemara, brew

like heat blisters where one floating continent
smashes against another. Ah, long perspectives!
—yet when all that unpleasantness went off

over the river in Trinity Term, tufts of flame
visible above Front Square, a rifle-crack brought
a tray of petrography slides down on my head:

chips and splinters of old landslips on the move,
snagged in my hair, the old earth under my feet
in an unseemly hurry all over again.

APPROACH TO THE CITY

Glimpsed among pines,
an absence marked.
Bucket of orange light

and a scatter
of ferries clearing the bay:
call that a city. Pines

tossing the breeze
from branch to branch,
pool of brown water,

whim of a parallax
view cancelling far
chimneys and traffic,

all that is not pines,
trees you can't
see the trees for.

City, wheedling child
in search of attention,
too brash to humour:

whispering pines,
too furtive to miss;
trunks tending

to earthward, already
asleep standing up.
Pine forest, butt

of old needles, trampers'
prints and branches
snapped back

into place behind us;
curtain after curtain
parted in search of

no stage but
a way among trees,
the city somewhere

below, our steps
tracing a path
and leaving no trace.

TUNNELS THROUGH THE HEAD

1

lapwing a lapwing standing on one leg
behind the strand and throwing its voice you
found an egg cracked and mottled like the new
moon at the end of the garden who knows
who you might be skulking face at the glazed
front-door preferring not to open to
the postman your mother or you now she
has died and you resemble her letters
piled up and unread would you be wanting
anything from the village greet no one
red-faced priest who gave you sweets as a girl
but mutter mutter to yourself in a
thin shrill voice its edge like the lapwing's egg
in your palm and cracked against your fingers

2

the mountains from the bedroom window smooth
are all breasts and pimples sharp are old teeth
you feel their breath on your neck father old
stony face back from the quarry tramping
decades of dust over the kitchen floor
in his boots from pebble-dashed house-front to
pebble-dashed grave by way of a dusty
solicitor to my only daughter
I leave this unfinished business of dust
not dispersed but thickening in the air
I leave these windows uncleaned old sealed tomb
of a house a stone through the window stays
where it falls grey granite veined with ghost tides
gone out to whispers of I leave I leave

3

or your voice shrapnelling down the phone with
fuck you screams old bollocks face screams I know
your game I ask you come back ten minutes
later and still droning on filthy stuff
never heard the like and the poor doctor
trying to call who's there get off the line

I'll have the Guards on you screams hang up go
stand on the beach where the little terns nest
gazing off towards the tunnels through the Head
the marvels of Victorian railway
engineering are we reduced to this
station gone an optional stop and a
woman prone by the boulders seen from the
train window a crow dead in its feathers

4

now shrill now near-mute do not adjust your
volume how must I strike you averting
your face in the laneway unstoppable
flow of over and over the old tune
father daughter hand in hand to the sea
again scatter of bay lights beckoning
hurry home through the long grass the back field
do you have playmates not today's little
miseries ringing the broken bell and
scattering chased from the garden crowing
exultant minions of scavenge rattling
the door-knob quick re-enter the eggshell
are you an excitable girl giggling
at the long decades ahead still unspoiled

5

or flat on a bench laughing at nothing
when asked to move on the accused began
to abuse passers-by in colourful
terms women expressed concern for get to
hell or if not laugh stony-faced blank whole
days without speaking to anyone pick
through the death notices he was no good
down the hatch with him faint rumble of bells
in the morning funeral masses of
broken glass shit sick and blood on your floor
or other days the floodtide in the head
stops eerie calm and the blue flowers blow
on the lane where donkeys ate your apples
such stillness have you a child is it you

6

does it shriek mutter cry unheard at night
your tale repeating you wake to its words
on your lips like finding the bathroom tap
running brown a pigeon dead in the tank
a rat in its juice the bathroom has no
mirror what must you look like imagine
observed or try the glass sliver you keep
in your bag never the whole wreck seen at
once eyes cheeks straw-wisps of hair a face in
anagram where might it ambush you next
in the butcher's window ruddy old side
of beef for the carving always the same
small shock of the pursed mouth turned away in
quick who's there turn away now confusion

7

memories are shredding what clings on all
starting over to shrieks and mutters of
out and away with you down the road in
rags and disgrace and the clank of your thin
plastic bags between the high hedges and
over the stones past the trains and low tide
will it stop here where only the bright stones
and the sea all bare and glitter the sun
on the tunnels through the Head where once but
these days no one but me father coming
and going where only a heron's eye
makes me out and shutting is gone in the
warm close dark is this where you're taking me
far faint last light drowning are we there yet

COLMCILLE'S FAREWELL

No horizon is not the better for want of you,
no storm at sea less welcome than your harbours.
You are the mistranscription in every manuscript,
the tuneless hymn intoned by the abbey dunce.
I would wish the Holy Mother the squealing of pigs
before the dull, click-clacking drone of your prayers.
You are a black cat's hairball on a high altar,
a rat making off with a consecrated host.
I stand on one leg like a crane to curse you,
I am squeezing my earlobe as I speak. Heavy
on my breast lies the salute I will offer
your vanishing shadow on the tide, and I am
the Bishop of Armagh asleep in a ditch, a drunkard
calling for bat's milk, a glutton dining on his
own fleas, and happy, in any world without you in it.

DRY DOCK

When you strip me down I will know our journey
to atoms together has started, when you flood,
float me in, and run dry. Are these the shallows?

This is where my bilge water curdles and spoils,
where each sandbank and reef pokes through
the chart the pilot spreads in the Minerva's

triangular room. To comic operas of sea shanties,
to an idling docker's flourish on the spoons,
reel in the foaming line I have slashed

through all our fabled tides. Belly full of toxins
swilling in an asbestos hold: no ghost ship comes
less haunted, no tally of journeys readier

for unlamented scrap. And not just journeys:
these seasick imperatives, warping pronouns,
ask only the lick of the blowtorch's sparks,

and they will have it. Another destiny than mine
awaits me. Softly into the dry dock's mud
behind its gates I feel my timbers sink and bloom.

DARK WATER

Form of formlessness that is snow:
that covets your outline all down the street
and follows you in the door; shaken
from shoes and overcoats but filling
back gardens all that week with trees

its own secret shape. Snow violence,
noisy and brash, toppling from roofs
and digging its isobars into the map,
like crampons. The small damp patch
in your soul has spread to the ceiling

and the back bedroom wall. Tonight
the stench pipe's mast will topple
under a roof-fall and Spring Bank
Cemetery's Greenland whaler captains
be icebound again. Yearning

in darkness for the word 'stillicide'
in your Hardy *Collected*, attic pipes
burst with enthusiasm; dark water's
blind eyes open where it falls
on vistas of brick dust and plaster.

A library is holding its breath
underwater, dedications paroled
from their promises in a sunburst
of inkspots relaxed into chaos
and pulp. Truth and beauty

overflow Keats's name rewritten
in water, encounter longer than usual
waits on the phone, a builder come
to poke at the roof while his mate chews
on a biscuit, all the dreary naiads

of a coldwater tap vomiting grit.
This page too is now underwater,

Narcissus dissolved in his pool:
blizzarding through holes in the roof
falls the furious indoor snow.

RAG AND BONE MAN'S MILD

after Baudelaire

> Poor old, tired old horse,
> patiently dragging what must
> feel like his own hearse.

Past the blue of the takeaway light grilling
flies for tea, where North Sea breezes roll in,
rattling the glass, out of some blind alley
where the tide of squalor rises daily,

comes, nodding his head, obscurely wise,
a rag and bone man, punching the walls as he goes,
flicking the law the finger on his patch
and holding forth to all from his royal coach.

Shouting the odds, he puts the world to rights,
gunning for wrong 'uns but looking out for mates:
huge on the throne and slicing the sky in half,
What a top bloke I am, he tells himself.

Canny lads, dodging social services,
do his bidding, as charming as they're vicious,
and chuck the fridges, tellies, bikes, on back,
all Bankside's indiscriminate bric-a-brac,

and so wind home, merry and victorious,
hailing their way down back-street terraces.
Every last tattoo's a campaign medal
for these veterans of old scrap metal,

with yards as rich as Ali Baba's cave
awaiting them and a fry-up on the stove,
and then a night on the tear to music pounding,
the lasses game, the pub-crawls never-ending.

Lubricating this daft life of theirs,
singing his exploits through their drunken roars

but needing only froth before he's crowned,
flows king mild, a rich brown river current,

the balm of idlers, stopping their mardy gobs
till chucking out time when they phone for cabs
to dump them home to sleep—but who needs sleep
when there's mild to drink, dark and true and deep!

INTERVIEW WITH A BINMAN

            Would you say rubbish
has always been important
            to you? Thinking back
to the rubbish you grew up
with, what first gave you the bug?

            What qualities do
you look for in a rubbish
            collection? Do you
work best in groups or alone?
Geoff Nobbs—genius or madman?

            How do you keep your
rubbish fresh? Are you worried
            it might run out? Do
you find it hard to let go
of? So what's next for rubbish?

            Tell me about some
of the rubbish you're working
            on now. When can we
expect to see this latest
rubbish of yours in the shops?

AIR STREET FUGUE

and it breathes and it twitches   and lives

an industrial eclogue
       rancid yet green

       odour of flowering skullcap

       the air powder-coated
                and shot-blasted

       into textures   of marvel

       circulated   recirculated
           sculpting themselves to my lungs

       here where green-jacketed
           young offenders

shackled in pondweed
       clear the drain

       and a green thought
abolishes all that's mard

          moorhens nest
       and the locked-in Alsatian

       plants the strawberry
of its snout   under the fence

       the padlocked cemetery
will not have you   alive or dead

       and what of it

       bury yourself in the air as you go
your steps repeat themselves   in your skull

you have been over this   way before now

there is only   so much   concrete
          left   to cover   the cracks

          when even   the tanner's yard's

          turning up   green

          the algae and oxidised pipework

                    festering green

of which   I ask you

          what   does it mean   to love
dereliction   if not
                              seeding
          this cherished boredom   with ever
more   of itself
          and only these few   stale blooms
to show   for it all

          the whimper   of who
but the sex fiends   users   and vagrants
          here beyond
                              street lights
                                        and CCTV
          or if not
                    if only
                              escape

          on a stray   cygnet's
                    trail of chevrons

          follow me

                    writ in water

          then into the briars

                    and asylum gained

with barely a splash

THE WANDERING ISLANDS

for Sam Gardiner

Unblocking a drain behind the privy
last St Ethelburga's day, the scullion
found a tiddy mun, small,
wizened, and bearded; taking it
for a Frenchman he caught the beast

a smart whack on the crown
before it loped off into the Ancholme,
pausing only to execrate
Cornelius Vermuyden, whoreson
Dutchman and drainer of fenlands.

Whims of an immemorial lutulence
these estuarine islands, soup bubbles
astir in the crook of the river's arm
where a dredger gives the sandbanks
the brush-off: slow-motion hide-

and-seekers of the floating centuries!
But—vengeance for the hog spirit—
Read's Island is sinking, reclaimed
tide by tide where a skeleton brickworks
returns to the clay and its deer-herd's

hoof-taps carry over the water.
Premature creatures of myth,
they stand among peewits and avocets
by the channel and drink; touched
by the 'bright light of shipwreck'

they will take to the water and swim.
Arriving too late to follow I make
my way to the water's edge and find
the currents, the sunlit shallows,
impenetrable in their wake.

KLANGFARBENMELODIE

                    Enter the haze
            a lake by Humber   orchestrated
        for woodwind and strings   (vole in the grass)
oboe and cello   (water rail's shriek)
                    slant sun   lighting the lake's
            touch paper   over its tidelines   (smew in the reeds)
        cloud of teeming   harmonies filtered
            through tympani and brass   (diving grebe)
        swelling   double-bass scrape   on the muddy bottom
            lacustrine synaesthesia in the key
        of bladder campion   and hawthorn scrub
    time signature   blood-spill twilight red
                Schoenberg's Third   Orchestral Piece   Op. 15
to the tune of   'I hate to see   the evening sun   go down...'
    and the water seeping   into your boots   where you stand
        and the song   on each harebell's tongue
    by puddle and lake   and the umber impassable sea
                asking only
                    carry me over

A BITTERING

Bíonn an fhírinne searbh

My arms are in up to the elbow in hops,
a bittering pot-pourri of Lincoln fields
coming apart in, and perfuming my hands.
We are measuring hops on a cast-iron scales
and admiring the barrels lying like drunks
under a pall of steam in the yard, reciting
extinct measure names to themselves: pottles,
pecks, fluid scruples. The malt in the vat
hides in its bubbles and froth, and memory
that intoxicant stirs in the mash tun.
Does it fancy rising, fermenting, returning
to life? The grains crack, water invades,
and—mashing, sparging, lautering—words
strain through a sieve in the mind, through all
that perfumes thick in the air restore, converting,
unselving me too.
               Pasteurised memory
seals the past in, a glass of tasteless lager
sipped from the adult table thirty years ago,
its fizz on the palate preserved and defunct,
leaving me wanting more, my thirst intact.
Down we go then, deeper under memory's
shifting currents, ready to foamy-whiten
my father's bristling moustache, coaxed
out from under the close shave of decades:
starveling ghost, its imprint retained
as long as the beer's slow-sinking head holds on,
just as the brew remembers the tank, the barrel,
the glass, the last plunge down our throats
into darkness. A child again, I consider
a pint of stout's snowy plunger pressing
the midnight flux all the way to the bottom,
ask permission to pierce its thick meniscus
with a straw. This photo album I revisit
through the lens of a toy box camera,
my blurry shots awash with anamorphic black,
white and cream: the contents of Bray harbour,

monochrome psychedelia of an old–style
TV on the blink, a long finish
from the dregs of childhood, capillaries
of froth climbing the glass and spilling over
the edge.
        The porthole into the bar mists over
as we work, hothousing us in odours
of mash, wort and fuggles. A farmer trades
our spent malt for a clutch of eggs, his roan
mare due a feast on our leavings, and time
ferments to the brew's present continuous:
I enter future memory, sharp and bitter, now;
the barmaid lighting the stove, the afternoon
drinkers coaxing sparks of conversation
from the cricket, or is it the rugby, or football;
years of this, gone and to come, remembered
from what other country, at what remove,
with what taste left in my mouth? Peering
into the barrel I find its contents already
ebbing to empty, sluiced like memory
along the drains and sewers of obsolescence,
pulsing subtler, stronger than the blood
diluted into grateful, dull amnesia,
needing the past but not me who was there.
The tide in Bray harbour sloshes in and out,
an empty glass sits in a lunar eclipse
of froth on the counter, and the lights come on
behind the porthole in the brewery window.
The beer is brewed, the living sediment
fermenting as I pour. The future drinks deep,
decanting us into sleep and the promise of next
year's hops, unsprouted still and the bitterest yet.

[UNTITLED]

i.m. P.R.

'After the childish
play-acting of recent years—
          the death mask cover,
the is-he-isn't-he works
of the "late" Peter Reading—

          the actual death
of the author comes as a
          refreshing return
to form, the silence leaving
no room for doubt, the loss of

          consciousness stark and
authoritative. Not for
          this Reading a fey
parting lament for the *[Note
to ed.: name of rare bird here]*

          or yet another
mawkish valedictory
          distich over an
*[Ed. again: expensive French
white wine]*. Entirely devoid

          of content, dying
suits our minimalist bard
          down to the ground. No
shortlist of deaths of the year
will be complete without it.

          In the wise words of
his dustjacket, this is a
          once in a lifetime
event, the outstanding death
of Peter Reading's career.'

REMNANT LAND

after Baudelaire

Poor people outside a new café... sentenced to death for a forgotten crime... the melancholy old widow before the Musard garden... the old acrobat... there are days when I sense myself so powerful that...

   [Hiatus in MS.]

Symptoms of ruin. Immense buildings. Many, one atop another, apartments, bedrooms, churches, galleries, staircases, cesspools, belvederes, lanterns, fountains, statues. —*Fissures, openings. Dampness seeping from a reservoir built under the sky.* —How to warn people and nations? —a word in the ear of the wisest.

On high a column cracks and its two ends work loose. Nothing has crumbled as yet. All henceforth issuelessness. I descend and come back up. *A labyrinth-tower. I never got out. I still live in a tower that will topple, a structure mined with a motion, a secret complaint.* —I enumerate, for my amusement, such a prodigious tally of stones, of marble, statues, walls, about to interpenetrate, splattered by that ramdam of skulls, human flesh and shattering bone. —I see such terrible things in my dreams that sometimes I would prefer not to sleep, if only I could be sure of escaping exhaustion.

Death as executioner. First outbreak of cholera at a masked ball in Paris, 1831. Death as friend. What sadness in solitary levity! Foundering sensation of crack-brained ruin. A monument to gaiety in the desert. Frivolity in abandon.

The local boutique, pale, anaemic, *café-au-lait,* like an old tobacconist's.

That shipwreck feeling.

DEATH ON THE BREEZE

after Frénaud

Nothing of those I have loved is forgotten.
They had sunk but their strength will return,
a fingertip touching my throat.
Under the dead weight of years, the evening light
regaining its splendour, they are scaled by a tear,
the beloveds lying undone by the spring.
All my childish lustre among the secretive
forms, letting them in between the big trees,
knocking them off their feet under
a passing cloud and a rainbow of impatience.

Off with them I go again, far below my face,
descending among the shadows that rule us,
cutting a dash here as they reveal me,
these dead, still quick if I am their memory,
their watcher or tomb—my own tomb too,
bedecked as is fitting
with a breezy grin for façade.

X

after Reverdy

To evade the lurking reef
that shadows me
that awaits the definitive step
to avoid ever turning again
over the love-slope deathlessly falling away
the love detaching itself from your guts
those free-verse unreasoning looks
and that portrait of you I would like to retouch
you tender-savage quick one in ardour's shadow
that look dissolving itself in the envious night
that look spitting tongues of jealous fire
in the evening dress that mantles the earth
at the moment when you go forth

far gone in despair
I will have buried my face in ice
the heart spiked by a thousand memorial fires
the reef of the future and death behind
and your smile too shallow
a moat
between us
words free
and the gestures withheld
of the winged hands extended in open sesame
until in the close weft dimly appears
the unheard-of wound whose salve I would be

MEMORIAL

In the Gaudíesque grotto of Eastern Cemetery's
columbarium, we found a crematee's plaque
cemented in upside down. How many turns
in our graves were we due before death pointed
underground again? Like an egg timer
I mentally resettled my dust as we tripped among
the old soldiers and plague victims, the council
strimmer marauding through the verges behind us.
Behind the prison wall there was Viking FM
for the category Bs, Her Majesty's pleasers
caught between the railway line to the docks
and the broken slabs pushed up against
the perimeter fence: heavy sleepers, there
for the duration, not about to wake now.

Hull, 2000–2012

ACCORDING TO LUCRETIUS

Up to the birds on the wing the Avernian lake
dispatches a toxic draught that leaks from a crack
in the earth, poisoning a corner of heaven;
no sooner does a bird pass over than a hidden
poison seizes and plunges it to its death
in the watery source below of the foul breath.
And as the fallen bird vainly flails and tosses
all life is drained from it by that halitosis.
Yet before it dies the foul breath drives it wild
with lust, for even in a place like this so soiled
and poisoned fresh life must be vomited forth,
such great perversity dwells there in the earth.
Another wile practised by the infernal lake
is to shatter the air between it and the flock
with its stench, leaving a pocket of pure vacuum.
Passing birds fly into it and meet their doom:
the beating of their wings slows and seizes up
and all their efforts leave them in a hopeless flap.
Dispossessed of the breezy luxuries of flight
they plummet earthwards under their dead weight,
and into the empty air around them as they fall
each bird scatters the wreckage of its poor wee soul.

IN MARRAKESH

The argan grove has goats in its hair,
swinging in the branches at night,
mild eyes aflutter, who strip
the nuts of their fruit, passing them
in dungy clumps for pressing down
to the oil you shake on our bread at sunset.

It is forbidden by law to disturb
a stork's nest: an imam who does so
is turned to a stork. A palace, let
the king think what he likes, is a pretext
for the storks' nests high on its walls,
to which each night you watch them return.

A sand-coloured cat becomes a remainder,
two blue eyes on a bed of sand,
a donkey a fly-kissed, dusty flinch
from a blow expected and not delivered,
the heat a violence turned on itself,
a lizard's tail come away in your hand.

And you, my witness, are the field whence
a child has driven the blank-eyed goats,
the nest on which the stork's legs buckle,
the dirty puddle that slakes the donkey
and cat's midday thirst then vanishes,
as a lizard vanishes, under a stone.

ADULTERY

from the Tamazight

Has Mahmoud married a third time in secret?
Brothers, so he would have us believe,
rolling his eyes and preening himself,
but I see him slip from his tent at night
in search not of some loose-sleeved beauty
but the storks that nest by the mosque,
singing to them while his wives sleep alone,
speaking their names like a young man in love.

IN THE MEDINA

The medina's noon
apocalypse of heat from on high
spends itself in the silver coin
of a blind beggar's eye.

SHORTS

THE NIGHT SHIP

The salt estranging sea between us raged and sickened
and through the porthole's film of condensation beckoned
a night ship's lights across the heaving dark I scanned
as one swimmer might for a second take another's hand.

THE FIRECREST

The firecrest weighs five paper clips
holding between them the sky together
but less than nothing weigh the stripes
igniting the bush where firecrests gather.

AVOCA RED

The scatter of kites I watched bank and soar
set off the late sun's crimson like a flare,
scarlet shot to rust and a sinking fire
where the river ran red with copper ore.

ROYGBIV

Carolina sky a paintball canvas where I traced
each last stripe on each last painted bunting's rainbow breast.

A SHRIKE

Viscera of broken song
threading the knots in her butcher's call
to barbed wire, steel-strung
death's-head chorus giving tongue
to the music of each catch, each kill.

PARADOX ELEGY

I remember my mother as a child.

TALE OF A HORSE

after Isaac Babel

It started with Savitsky taking Khlebnikov's white stallion.

Khlebnikov was given a black mare instead, but pined for his stallion.

So Khlebnikov wrote to headquarters, who said, Give him the horse
back.

Off he rode to get it and found Savitsky shacked up with some Cossack
girl.

Do you know who I am?, asked Khlebnikov. It says here to give me my
horse!

Do you want a piece of this, said Savitsky, waving his pistol. Get lost!

Off rode Khlebnikov to the Chief of Staff who said, I dealt with this
earlier.

So Khlebnikov sat down and wrote a letter saying, That's it, I'm off.

On and on it went, saying how much he missed his stallion.

You idiot, said the commissar, come and have dinner; it's just some
horse.

But he threw himself on the ground saying, Go ahead, shoot me.

All he wanted was his damned horse.

And off he went, and that's how we lost him.

I saw a lot of myself in Khlebnikov.

The whole world to us was a meadow in May criss-crossed by women
and horses.

THE PRESIDENT OF PLANET EARTH

И с ужасом
Я понял, что я никем не видим,

Что нужно сеять очи,
Что должен сеятель очей идти!

And with horror
I understood—no one could see me.

I would have to sow eyes.
My task was to be a sower of eyes!

You were Xodasevich, I was Xlebnikov,
where the Cyrillic X marked the spot
and the Café Iskra rang with the forced laugh
of crewcut Futurists come to drink and plot.

That was the year Natalia fell for Boris,
who loved Anna, who loved Sergei in vain,
pince-nez'd, married Sergei she would embarrass
with harebrained sonnets trying to explain.

Chai-cup storms within a storming shark pool!,
where Acmeists would shout down party placemen,
Old Believers noisily talk bull,
and the silent ones were always secret policemen.

Do you remember our local Mayakovsky,
less a 'cloud in trousers' than a rain shower,
piddling revolution from on high
while we looked for an umbrella we could share?

Or our Esenin, signing with his blood
each update from his daily bust-up/love-in,
or bumptious, bourgeois Pnin who sat and blubbed,
poor man, how he had 'nofing left, nofing, nofing'?

But is that the fee-fi-fo-fum of the Kremlin
mountaineer approaching, scaling the onion

domes in Peter's Square? Your fear and trembling
at the age to come can never come too soon.

I still see the snow outside the Winter Palace
that January morning, splashed with sickening
raspberry ripple. The bloodlust never cloys,
but the blizzards of the lost will have their reckoning.

Hang more Professors!, Lenin telegrammed
drily to some Junior Dean of slaughter.
I've seen the dead dug up and altars grimed
with blood and shit by soldiers racked with laughter.

The show of red flags billowing in that heady
air like Isidora Duncan's scarf
choked as much as swaddled any Mayday
victory march declaring none would starve.

The emotions, it appears, are unskilled workers.
I never yet saw a quatrain stop a bullet,
but I've a fond delusion that recurs
a poet-king will one day top the ballot—

not any old poet, but Viktor Vladimirovich!
Otherwise swap a despot for a bard
and learn too late you're stuck with one of each,
and the execution warrant as high art.

Have you *seen* that rank Ossetian's doggerel,
targeting his words like a firing squad,
who couldn't find a rhyme for bugger all
and scans like a tank battalion on parade?

My favourite fruit is eyeballs, I still hear
my ravenous interrogator boast,
who kept his belly full and conscience clear,
my 'one-half Nero, one-half Jesus Christ'.

Still, inspiration, I wouldn't call you a gent
banging on the door at midnight, shining

a torch in my face like a Cheka agent,
you the sinned against and I the sinning,

crushing our offspring come the dawn like lice.
And yet they worship me and swarm back nightly
pleading filthily with me for their lives,
I, my poems' larval God-almighty!

I've also studied
               the staircase
                             lineation
you use, Vlad,
               though seasick
                         I confess,
or landsick
               at its all-out
                         tumbling motion,
like the stop-go
               nude in Marcel
                         Duchamp's canvas.

I'm a Rodchenko montage, Lily Brik-
meets-brontosaurus, beauty and the beast;
I'll bankrupt your aesthetics, go for broke,
a thundering slap in the face of public taste.

Calling down for room service I got
the year 1913 ('Is that the future?'),
and felt the time-lag give me it right in the gut,
knocked into next year like a prize fighter.

In an abstruse mathematical equation
I came upon the formula for war
in Japan and famine in the Volga Basin
and tried to pass my findings to the Tsar.

Take the circumference of a drop of blood
expressed as a ratio of the equator
and you've the secret, world-traversing code
that carries me from inner space to outer.

Alchemo-numerologically, nine
contains the answer to the *kulak* crisis.
The end to war's an undiscovered prime
of which, innumerates, we have but traces.

I who understand the language of birds
have risen up against the bully-boy sun,
hitched a lift on the comet-tails of words
and planted myself on his throne to pulse and shine.

Glossolalic pentecosts of trans-sense
(transmagnificanjewbangstantiality!)
putting to the sword the dragon one-sense
(zaumnostomniumhorrorshowreality!).

O tundra, steppe or taiga landscapes lacking
all horizon, face without a profile;
o winter sun these latitudes will blacken
until all-conquering seeds of light prevail!

Wandering the fly-blown road to Persia
I thought of you, Prometheus, on your rock,
served up for the tyrant gods' sick pleasure
in a soup of your own loins with liver stock

to that insatiable vulture Thou Shalt Not.
No guts need spill when I redeem mankind:
my brain's a honeycomb that all can eat
and live in too, a self-devouring hive mind.

Spying myself in a reservoir in Baku
I flinched from my Rasputin-like long hair.
Rublev's God, it's time that I forsook you;
your word of God's one cosmic-sized *longueur.*

The flame I light needs sacred mirth to fan it:
that's why I snort at *The Brothers Karamazov.*
The eternal silence of those infinite
spaces makes me want to laugh my ass off!

Ecky-thump way-I-tell-'em never-sunnier
tittyfalarious I-say-I-say tee-hee-hee!
Bitter/hollow/mirthless nothing-funnier-
than-unhappiness down-the-snout *smekhachi!*

All Russia is to me a living grammar
book and its map a verb I conjugate.
The dictionary I ride like a gray mare,
surveying my words like any head of state.

I dream of single-letter poems, each
an atom of the Slavic brain writ large —
my nano-epics *Kh*, *Sh*, *Ch* and *Shch*,
the diary of a trip to Prague called *Ř*.

Truly I am the president not just
of Russia but of Planet Earth, whose mission's
to transform the greatest and the least
of us from earthlings into pilgrim Martians.

Today you 'forgot to hang yourself', Kruchenykh.
I put a gun to my head and forgot to shoot.
My speed of thought's already supersonic.
I'll sew you a thinking cap from a winding sheet.

The skull to me was always a space helmet.
There's a planet named for me, 3112,
I yearn for like a melancholy soulmate;
I'll start the rocket, Russia, if you come too.

Yet what if at journey's end waits some rough beast
to whom my demon love's still too low-key?
'O Russia, my wife!', whose kisses not I taste
but one more psychosexually Blok-y?

Revolutions eat poets, swallow them whole.
Somewhere in the Kremlin sewer there lurks
regurgitated, drowned and damned, the sole
surviving scrap of all my vanished works.

Isaac, you'll pioneer a whole new genre,
silence, but there's no dumb-show dumb enough,
no batting eyelid tics that don't spell 'goner'
in Morse code to your NKVD oaf.

And Isaac, not forgetting that tale of yours
I'm in where that blackguard takes my stallion—
my beauty bow-legged from some Cossack's arse—
while I end up deserting, weeping, wailing,

and over the noise of battle comes the motto,
louder than bombs, cannons and my curses,
'The whole world to us was as a meadow
in May crisscrossed by women and horses.'

Time the barber is Sweeney Todd-meets-Occam.
I speak with the clairvoyance of Armageddon:
Boris, beware a telephone call from Stockholm,
Osip, don't get on that train to Magadan.

Kruchenykh, you'll pant on to the Prague Spring—
Janáček erupting into doo-wop,
flower-power Communism—but not quite long
enough to look us up on Ubuweb.

Ah, internet! where all our dreams come true,
where Ron Silliman blogs for pure love
of the post-avant, and tweets and podcasts too,
and I am facebook friends with Marjorie Perloff.

They like me will have had their share of ills
on the road to permanent Futurity—
tenure committees, Billy Collins' book-sales,
ripped-up tickets for that Swedish lottery.

Time is the breach that only time can mend,
the beating core of the caesium atom.
Eternity is to live in the present moment:
there and only there am I at home.

Byzantium's golden groves could not compete
with this desert of the real bleached to lead
where the hills ring to my Gul-Mullah's trumpet,
my white wings broken, my poor brain full of blood,

my poor brain wrecked on the reef of the world's 'No';
where I hurl my words at the sky to no avail,
buried under rockslides by their echo
snagged on my skull like a gramophone needle.

A child on the beach, I built my sand-castles
from the total grains of sand of human bliss
and skimmed rhymes out to sea, frail vessels
on trade routes far beyond all profit and loss.

Now otherworldly as you like a breeze
begins to trace the contours of my death mask,
my laments hurry me downhill like skis,
and life is a chewed and spat-out sunflower husk.

That was the year Natalia fell for Sergei,
who loved... who had a fling with... who went mad...
But what are you doing, Russia, after the orgy
of history, if you're still in the mood?

You were Khodasevich, I was Khlebnikov;
am Khlebnikov, I am that vessel still
through whom all that was promised, broken off
mid-word, will yet arise in living steel.

OBLIVIA

after César Péru

'Canta, lluvia, en la costa aún sin mar!'

Bronze-by-gold sun on a flint-knife
sculpting obsidian, on the snarl of a god

who eats dead babies. How many
traditions have I invented, and lost

golden ages compelled into
existence to dignify the slow

afternoons sliding into the whims
and anomie of a quarter past four

in Trujillo? Never enough, chronicler-
custodian that I am of these testy late Springs.

Silver-by-tungsten sun on the fork
of a notary eating tripe in the window

of the Simón Bolívar Hotel
and the lazaretto bell chiming the hour.

All that febrile, hurricane year
our pronouns shifted uneasily

under our blistered feet, the dawn's
first-person Quechua plural

as we descended the hills to work
in the sugar plantations shifting

by mid-morning to an imperative
Spanish singular whispered through

the venetian blinds, in whose voice but yours.
Watch for me where your legs await

the moment of ideal length in their shadows,
on the terrace at noon. (Never

have I seen such lovely crossed teeth,
the alpaca thinks of her mate.)

Wait for me where death rolls
the dice and they turn up snake eyes

in the sockets of an old skull
children kick round the graveyard,

tin-miners' children, their eyes the colour
of pewter, and this is our little apocalypse,

where everything dies and stays just the same.
Our wars of saline inertia, our over-excitable

avant-garde at work on the world's
first sonnet that is also a grand piano

and sewing machine. When you turned
the key in my office door, I knew

you had come to talk about poems.
Our teeth behind their mumbled syllables

rattle snugly as my key in its wards,
your last touch on the handle casting adrift

all hope of the coast from these far limits.
Recto and verso, our shores reach

for each other, their dream of meeting
violent as upturned books swept

in a rain of papers from the table
and snapping shut on the floor.

THE ILLUSTRATED VERSION

Oh no! Mr Balloon, my one true friend, is getting away!
Cat's-bum mouth of alarm, face haloed in comedy

ectoplasm; an exclamation mark huge in the air
like a blimp while Mr Balloon recedes to the white dot

of a turned-off TV. Empty yard times three, each panel
twice the size of the last. This feature you may read

left to right or up and down as you choose. Kids!
Impress schoolmates by ending sentences short

of the right-hand margin. This is 'poetry' and all
your friends are doing it. Also available in endword-

soundalike form. For personal remarks
see ISBN page, for radioactive core

of unspent youth, let's see where this promising
masturbation storyline takes us. Save me,

world's most inadequate superhero! Or fail
to save me with pathos and a comedy outfit

pulled too tight on your paunch. The last time
Uncle Abe was here he just sat by the window

all day shouting at clouds, landlocked in a
perpetual Omaha of the mind.

Learn humming noises quickly and efficiently.
Free with this issue self-assembly actual time machine.

(Not actual time machine.) Note in the corner of
this frame the sadly withered, ignored Mr Balloon,

fallen to earth. Mr who? Flashback,
dream sequence, life on Mars. Invasion

of the fifty-foot women; most important character
shown only from the ankles down. And yes,

your words are physically present to me in the air
as you speak. Last leaf standing on the sycamore

by the silo takes two pages to fall.
Man on deathbed is his own grandfather, father,

self, and dreams of a misspent life, the life
still to come. A last thought bubble

unmoors from my brow, floats off over the freeway:
Th-th-thanks for everything! the henceforth

nameless man-child waving after it as it goes.

      after Chris Ware

ACCORDING TO LUCRETIUS

With bulls too the Carthaginians waged war
on their foes, and not just bulls but wild boar.
Using an armed handler to keep the beast in line
some went further again, with a fierce lion.
But pity the man who thinks that he can keep
a lion on a leash and it not give him the slip.
Blood up, they'd rampage here and there and sow
chaos among the squadrons, friend and foe,
their shaking, horrent manes and then their roars
enough to put the wind up any horse.
In vain their riders urged them with the snaffle,
the sight of angry she-lions proved too awful:
pouncing from nowhere into their victims' faces,
landing on their backs and ripping them to pieces,
catching hold and wrestling them to the ground
then pinning them by the gaping, mortal wound
that they'd inflict with grim bites and slashing claws.
Their own side the bulls would trample and toss
in the air, and horses they would run right through
with their horns, impaling the creatures from below
then pawing the dust with menacing intent.
The boars also turned their horns on foe and friend
and washed the weapons lodged in them in blood.
Cavalry tumbled, infantry died where they stood.
The panicked, bolting horses tried to veer
to safety or, rising up, would paw the air
in vain: on every side the earth rang out
and shook with the collapsing horses' weight.
If anyone doubted that these beasts were wild
before, the proof lay on the battlefield
in carnage, uproar, terror, anarchy.
Nothing will keep such killers, broken free,
from dealing death all round with no one spared,
just like elephants, badly battle-scarred,
that stagger and stamp down hard on anyone
in their way. As if they care what side he's on!

FOR CLAUDE DEBUSSY

Pink candyfloss clouds of the *fin-de-siècle*
raining fat-fingered chords and ragtime jokes
from Gallic heaven on this morning's grade VIII

piano practice; a cathedral rising out
of a lake and a left-hand tenth I stretch
unbroken. Should we write only for God,

like Palestrina, write only for the waggish
ice-cream-licking pug approaching us
on the Boulevard Clichy? A cat's paws

on the keyboard test the difference
between *pp* and *ppp* in time
to the washerwoman's heels clicking

a habanera over the tiles, out of time with
my mother in the next room humming the tune.
We reject sweaty Wagnerian vehemence

and obligatory thunderstorms; we defend,
to the last drop of our *café noir,* Edgar
Allan Poe, the key of B♭ major,

and the interrupted cadence. Tickling
away at *Des pas sur la glace* over cocktails
at the North Pole, 'Have you met...?'

I begin, when the ice under Satie's
feet gives way, cutting him off mid-sentence.
'*Zut alors!*' tuts a duchess breaking a nail

as, fresher than icebergs, slier than
my breath freezing into a beard, my busy
fingers course with your warm, wise blood.

SELF-PORTRAIT AS WOMAN READING A LETTER

Meet me by the canal, you said. Very funny.
The man on the street was swigging lighter-fuel
or beer, I couldn't tell which, until flames
began to sprout from his lips. Hidden
among the Rijksmuseum's treasures
was the work of an Old Master who paints
empty church interiors and nothing
besides. Meet me by the bridge with the bicycles,
I suggested. That joke only works first time,
you replied. Everyday Dutch life as fine art—
this doorway, that window—our improvised
theory ascribed to the birth of capitalism
from the wars of religion. Where is
the cardinal in this scene, the Borgia prince
concluding a treaty with a nod of his head?
Staring up from his courtyards in Delft,
Pieter de Hooch depicted the daylight
with the lightest of paint, namely pure white.
During the great gunpowder explosion
that claimed his life, Fabritius's goldfinch
was briefly startled from its inn-sign
before resettling. Venturing into the Domkerk
I found legions of stationary cyclists
all down the nave receiving the blessing
of the bicycles and pedalling hard.
A young woman struck by a bicycle
had hauled herself off the road and lay there,
moaning and calling for aid. Our theories
on the Dutch East Indies proved full of holes.
The boathouse lunette window faced north
in search of the light it would never catch.
When satisfied with his paintings, Vermeer
would take a pin and carefully prick a hole
in the canvas to announce they were finished at last.

FOR TEREZA LÍMANOVÁ, PAINTER

texture   boundary   movement
a fence snakes   between void
and void   a ladder no one climbs
hangs on the wall

this canvas shows   evidence
of recent human   departure
and frames   within frames
an absence   between two gate-

posts glimpsed   over a shoulder
glimpsed   from a tram window
more than bindweed   slips
through the cracks   in the pavement

a two-headed streetlamp
is a seedpod   and red
is a wound   light leaks
from the low sun   and clings

indelible   looking is writing
letters on street-signs   are power-
lines   branches   vectors
knitting and fused

how hiddenness stays
unmissable
is a revelation   you take
the simplest of walks   to the end

of the street   stop for breath
at the edge   of the possible
and go   on your way
in no   particular direction

FOR PIERO DI COSIMO

Canvas is expensive and one who wastes
canvas on paintings not of the Bishop
of Bobo or the Countess of Caca
is an irresponsible person and you
are that person, abominating
the coughing of men and the chanting
of friars and making fifty boiled eggs
at a time. Vitruvius is telling you
how language was born: *when the trees*
caught fire, the men of old found
how pleasant the warmth was,
and trying to speak of this gave forth
sounds with differing intensity,
making customary by daily use
these random syllables. 'More beast
than man', said Vasari: pyrophobe
who would set Eden ablaze and send
the beasts stampeding towards us,
lions, bears and aurochs punished
for not wanting rid, they too, of heaven
on earth. The forest is a furnace
but in the middle distance a goat
and deer with human faces pause
and ask themselves what to do: what
bodies, whose faces to wear,
they wonder, nature wonders,
flush with the wisdom of utter defeat
as a peasant of genius spells
'f – i – r – e, fire' for the first
time and the whole world burns down.

AN EXECRATION

Given the existence of plagues of eels and bloodsuckers in Lake Leman,
cursed by the Bishop of Lausanne and the learned doctors of
    Heidelberg,
the homicidal bees condemned at the Council of Worms, the petition
of the inhabitants of Beaune for a decree of excommunication against
    certain
noxious insects called hurebers, a kind of locust or harvest-fly—
given, further, the trial of the weevils of St Jean-de-Maurienne lasting
over eight months, with due attention to the protocol of cases brought
against caterpillars, to the custom of writing letters of advice to rats,
the writs of ejectment served on them, and the rhyming rats of Ireland;
and, further, Egbert, Bishop of Trier, having previously anathematized
the swallows which disturbed the devotions of the faithful and
    sacrilegiously
defiled his head and vestments with their droppings, and exulted
in scandalous unchastity during his sermons; in spite of the vermifugal
    efficacy
of St Magnus' crozier and accompanying papal execratories, all sorts
of animals, a cock burned at the stake for the unnatural crime of laying
an egg, an ox decapitated for its demerits, all manner of sweet
and stenchy beasts, are observed to persist in their heretical obduracy,
irrational and imperfect creatures, though notified, admonished and
    commanded
to depart from the habitations of man, notices to this effect being
    posted
on trees that all guilty parties may read; and whereas it has been
urged that brute beasts that they are, the field-mouse, locust, mole,
ass, mule, mare, goat, snail, slug, weevil, turtle-dove, pig, cow and
    bull,
are lacking immortal souls (that they might be damned), they lack not
indwelling spirits, otherwise demons and imps of Satan, of which
they are the visible form, so that it is the demon and not the beast
that suffers in the beaten dog and squeals in the butchered pig;
a vile and lowly specimen of which genus art thou, the accused,
standing trotters against the dock before me now, that did wilfully
last Tuesday fortnight throw the swineherd's son to the ground,
mangling his ears and cheeks, for which crime having first been
    dressed
in a velveteen waistcoat as is our custom and the executioner furnished

with a fresh pair of gloves, you will be conveyed to the town square and there without benefit of clergy be hanged by the neck until dead and your body thereafter displayed for the improvement of your fellow filth-dwelling sinners. Do you have anything to say for yourself?

BIOGRAPHIA LITERARIA

Being a straight man gave Alfie plenty
of issues to work through in his poems.
The first praise Bethany got meant
that bit more coming from me. Only
at the launch did Cathal notice his name
had been misspelled on the cover.
It's not a competition, Declan told
Eveline. You've won your first competition,
Eveline congratulated Declan.
This next poem's for my enormous cock
of an ex-husband, Freya would announce
to nervous giggles. Everyone loved George
and now he's remembered only for that one line.
Thinking of slipping into the river
Harry—typical Harry—still purchased
a parking permit. Ian proved
an enthusiastic reviewer of his peers.
Prize-win by prize-win, the world
finished Jack off. Two book dedications
have just been informed Kate and Leo
are no longer together. On balance,
Mo's fling with his editor worked out
just fine. Niamh recently published
her keenly-awaited seventh collection,
perhaps her finest to date. Freezing at
the microphone, Oliver walked offstage
and never came back. Not another
honorary degree, groaned Phyllis.
I reject the heteronormative, gendered
lyric said Queenie, to great acclaim.
You wouldn't believe how feminist I am,
said Richard. Slowly Sarah got used
to being the only non-white face in the room.
Your student days at Trinity were important
to you, weren't they, interviewers would ask
Tara. These days, I find, all I care about
is the quality of light on the kitchen wall,
said Una. I can still change, said Victor.
I have someone who handles all that

for me, said Will. We tried to help
Xander but in the end there was nothing
we could do. Yolanda still pops up
on my feed now and then. Zoe died young.

THE RUMOURED EXISTENCE OF ELSEWHERES

The island behind the island behind the island.
The loch with no name robbing us of ours too.
The waterfalls flowing backwards and up in the wind.
The ferry circling at anchor like a dog in a back garden,
the ferry that runs only in winter, and then
on the Sabbath. The flag of an unknown nation,
wistfully displayed. The island whose shape
must grace every wall, tea mug and biscuit box,
until life is only the island, shape of a
spasming crayfish, shape of a gannet
in a top hat. The murmuring revelation
of this, this patch of gorse here.
My roustabout nights, my subtle apocalypse.
The bridge we built broken, the rumoured
existence of elsewheres. The winding
stair that reached to the sky.
My breath on the window, reversed.
A pine marten licking its paws
by the duach. The island
in front of the island in front
of the island. Here was
a one-track road that led
back on itself over and over
to ever-new destinations. Here
was a one-track destination
leading only and
infinitely to itself.

Mull

KEEN

Under the plane's giant white-tailed eagle-wing
where flitting Sweeney's final teardrop fallen
petrified to Ailsa Craig, flitting all alone
myself, I fancied that I heard a great auk calling.

Clearing the shore, I found the empty quarter waiting—
snow-patches in the Cairngorms clinging on
as though the rigging of the sky had tumbled down
and tangled on the peaks, some rare and downy thing.

And where the plane turned east-south-east I thought
to linger straining for the cries mistaken for
a witch of that last stray bewildered auk.

But strain as I might for echoes from the western shore—
the thresh of the huge wings caught in stillborn flight—
its keen was lost in the propellers' *och och och.*

WARM FRONT

Heavy with Christmas snow a granite sky bore down
on the windscreen as its streams began to harden
into ice now warmth was gone and ice was certain.

Of all we'd left behind we pausing asked for pardon
while over the road around us closed a snowy curtain
and shouldering its drifts we warmed to such a burden.

UNPACKING A LIBRARY

i.m. D. O'D.

>   Someone today will
> not be writing soon-to-be
>   cancelled cheques, eating
> a last sandwich, or circling
> posthumous calendar dates—

>   time unfillably
> idling instead in your wake
>   in a rented house
> and not one book of yours to
> hand, not a borrowed word in

>   explanation of
> death catching your eye. Today
>   for the living will
> not mean a last look at the
> world or weather forecasts for

>   their own funerals
> but survival's non-event,
>   mute spirit haunting
> an empty cage, unspoken
> for in so much voicelessness;

>   until, dark-garbed, two
> removers come to the door
>   bearing load after
> load of—steady there—M, N,
> O'Callaghan, Conor, O'

>   Callaghan, Julie,
> O'Driscoll, Ciaran and—ah,
>   so there you are then—
> O'Driscoll, Dennis, lifted
> carefully free of the box.

LOW FLIER

A helicopter is filling my windscreen,
greedy for the nearest soft landing.
A window becomes a cat's face, turned,
and deer are grazing on the front lawn,

greedy for the nearest soft landing
when they jump the fence for cover,
deer grazing on the front lawn
between one clearing and the next.

When they jump the fence for cover
they must be visible from the chopper
between one clearing and the next
under the flashing red safety light.

I must be visible from the chopper;
everything goes somewhere to hide,
but flushed out by the safety light
I hunch, found and tracked in its flicker.

Everything goes somewhere to hide
but the chopper is filling the windscreen.
I hunch, found and tracked in its flicker,
and a window becomes a cat's face, turned.

A PSEUDOCOUPLE

Callum and Hamish: two herring gulls
you'll recognise at once from their calls.
'Callum' says Hamish, 'Hamish' says Callum,
eyeing each other up with the calm
of two gunslingers facing off
then making their peace with a raucous laugh.
'You again for the millionth time',
the first and millionth time the same:
'Hamish', 'Callum', 'Callum', 'Hamish',
don't blame me if it gets a bit sameish,
like Didi and Gogo with their 'Come here
till I embrace you', like Mercier and Camier,
dancing and bowing before getting down
to dipping for chips in the nearest bin.
Like Bouvard and Pécuchet, I mean
Statler and Waldorf, Shem and Shaun—
two philosophers on a field trip,
two hecklers shouting from the rooftop,
two twins warring for every scrap
of mouldy batter burger bap.
Or do I mean Morecambe and Wise for the mix
of tuneless songs on top of the jokes,
or Keats and Chapman, that pun-struck pairing
their banter lost on the hard of herring,
or Scotus Eriugena and Duns Scotus,
whose avian gospel long has taught us
the Holy Spirit's grace is spread
in streams of guano discharged on my head,
or Wallace and Bruce, heroes aa ken,
wi' a flash o' Saltire blue in their e'en.
Yet none of these has swooped to land
on the verge where you eat from my hand,
and we've the sun on Don and Dee—
boats spangled on the far North Sea—
so you're the show, and all you bring
of ruckus, blather, wit and song.

BENNACHIE TO CLACHNABEN

Paps I'd laud in song and story
across the Mearns and the Garioch:
above the snowline, through the haar,
cries one to t'other, Are you there?—
Bennachie to Clachnaben
and likewise echoed back again;
stretched along the lazy beds,
crowns of buzzards round their heads,
where Don and Dee each follow courses
bundled over sheer drops harsh as
winter north-northeasters blown
past Fair Isle to our frost-bound lawn.
Where beaker people warred with Picts
and Celts' and Romans' gore was mixed,
history's a page some march on
and others scratch around the margin
voicelessly in cultic runes
that calcify on standing stones—
an age usurped by Christ and Lug
still keeping watch from every crag.
The blood-red of the painted field—
vain tribute to the gods that failed—
dilutes to present greeny-gray
(the word *glas* glosses either way),
and where the hulking tors might end
and city start nae sailors kennt
in gurly waters, or couldna dee
without the sight of you at sea:
skyline savage as the grin
of the final grey wolf hunted down!
Savage Piranesi dungeons
of the city's close-drawn confines!—
through which shrills the sharp sea breeze
and, mourning for their failed embrace,
clean as a hawk's beak snapping bone,
Bennachie's cry to Clachnaben.

BROCK

Breac the brock
laid broken-backed
by the side of the road,
white & black
pattern stitched
& unstitched,

unpacked, unpicked.
My Alan Breck,
dashing Jacobite
gone hither & yon
at his master's call
& beck: towering

broch reduced
to a brick of a thing;
there when I drive
to work & when
I drive back, dead
weight tipped

like so much bruck.
The Celts fancied
the god Apollo
a burrowing brock:
the healer god,
great sea badger—

removing which
hard-shoulder bric-
a-brac the council
call 'uplifting'
work, but oh
the ache

as sessions of winter
& spring snow
come and go

with still no curtain
of soil drawn over
poor brock's back.

TREE TO TREECREEPER

A slow-descending raindrop
　　　inches leaftip to tip
　　　　　from treetop

to where root-dwellers sup
　　　and passes coming up
　　　　　the tiny hop

o' my thumb of your treecreep—
　　　a spiralling sweep
　　　　　without stop

of my thick skin and frozen sap,
　　　woken from its winter sleep
　　　　　to your *tap tap.*

CROSSBILL

Berry aslant a mismatched bill.
Gulp and trill. Through crossed teeth
and echoing yours my woodnotes spilled
        while you sang still.

Blood-red shed by the crossbill-scythe
where the blood-red breasts rebuffed the gale,
a true note in each crooked mouth

carrying up and down the hill
on each far-transported breath
(the crossbill's beak will never seal)—
        carrying still.

AT FOOTDEE

Little ringed plover,
shivering into your grey
and white pullover.

ROUNDS

i.m. Sam Gardiner

1

The bus-driver who picked me up in town
had driven me in that same morning, amusing
himself while I did my rounds doing
his own small extra round of the empty roads.

2

Confusing my entries and exits in Gretna once,
mistaking a wedding for a funeral,
I learned the first and last houses in Scotland
were the same place, saving me all sorts of time.

3

The plan was, talk you round to stay for just
one more before we parted and off you went
for a bus over the Humber Bridge, thoughts
of driving the long way round long gone, historical.

4

Heaven, like the ruins of Rome, is full
of cats chasing their tails and sorely let down
when they catch them, wondering what remains
if not to swallow themselves whole and vanish.

5

Needing to fact-check your obituary
and finding myself with no other contact
email address than yours I thought I'd try it
and sure enough you wrote back straight away.

6

As we talked, the bus for your funeral over
the bridge backfired as though firing off rounds
and—tiring of my claims that Purgatory
goes round and round—the driver left without you.

ECLOGUE

Where Kintore stallions raced and Arthur Johnston
saw, not Donside but the Pelopponesian
hippodrome, Apollo blessed the nation
with fresh eclogues for each tree and stone.

Soft murmur of Renaissance Latinists
alongside courtly French and teuchter Gaelic,
or high-toned bugling of the Grampian elk
on Munros where the capercaillie nests,

trail our long-horned cows across the sheilings
of the ages, who harvest onto scribal
vellum skaldic ballads, Oghamic rubble,
stramashes fought for women, crowns and shillings.

No forest trail or visitors' centre
finds the paths that we inscribe in time,
and in whose sodden cover we reclaim
lost realms of '45er and dissenter.

Receding under hazelraw, our same
few kirkyard names lose legibility—
Fraser, Gordon, Watt—and all our fealty
passes to the soft slate sunk in loam,

whence flows, and to which returns our song.
Grey that framed us living frames us gone
who lay cut flowers on granite, as though the stone
itself were what we'd honoured all along.

SIR THOMAS URQUHART CONSIDERS THE TONGUES OF MEN, AND WHETHER ONE MIGHT NOT BE FASHIONED ABOVE ALL OTHERS PERFECT

Notwithstanding it has been established by his late Majesty
that children raised in perfect silence teach themselves Hebrew,

& harried by interruptions to my studies (marching south
from Turriff we took and lost the fair city of Aberdeen,

while at Worcester I carried my papers into battle & suffered
their most grevious loss: all my quinternions—used for

the packing up of figs in the marketplace—gone!); more
tremendous yet than this, a vision has been vouchsafed me

of a dialect above all others perfect. Alone among places
the dwellings, temples, and dens of Cromarty have retained

their Greek names of old, awaiting only the perfection
of human speech that we might enter the New Arcadia.

Should I utter a word never before heard in this tongue,
it is understood readily by all; in fourscore words and ten

it conveys whole folios at once. There is no English word
but I will translate it into another of the same length,

employing identical letters, daydreaming the while
of a bald-pated fellow I saw in Madrid who believed

he was Julius Caesar. Daydreaming that I am Julius Caesar,
Alexander the Great, Isaiah the Prophet, the Prince of Denmark,

all conversing most sagely in the tongue I have fashioned.
The which I did roar at my equerry amid the skirmish

at Worcester, to gather my scattering papers, to no avail.
My studies beset by damnable intermittences (the trumpeting

---

of clergymen, their scolding more like a tripe-seller's wife than good counsel). The which tongue I am at last resolved

to unveil. Which I shall now unveil. Which I shall shortly unveil: shortly, which is to say never. Which I shall never unveil.

1655

ROGER HILTON, *NOVEMBER '64*

'We either touch or do not touch'
across the tides that circulate
from Cornish sound to silver north;
in nets of colour, past the Firth,
we find our misplaced eyes too late
in deeper-than-deep blues you catch.

A spar, a prow, a rock, the sun:
they are not fixed but follow courses
framing patterns known to brush
and nib alone, now smooth, now harsh;
take our tributes with our curses
who helpless face the storm-waves down.

A man is gathering limpets from
the shore past which the trawlers scud
like fairground nags that rise and fall,
gauzed in the haar through which I feel
our ruin drawn tight like a coat
with not one light to see us home.

Sydney Graham reach me a hand.
I read behind the forms a tale
that falls away and leaves the forms,
the floods of light that burst their frames
and bursting launch the canvas sail
I still believe can find your strand.

THREE THINGS

i.m. Diarmuid Ó Gráinne

Three things that constitute an artificer.
Three signs of wisdom, three signs of folly.
A deer shedding its horn, a wood shedding
its leaves, cattle shedding their coat. A drop
of blood, a tear-drop, a drop of sweat.
Three smiles that are worse than sorrow,
three silences that are better than speech.
The darkness of mist, the darkness of night,
the darkness of a wood. Three unfortunate
things for a man. Plenty and kindliness
and art. The shout of distributing, the shout
of sitting down, the shout of rising up.
Three fewnesses that are better than plenty.
Patience, closeness, prophecy. Three speeches
that are better than silence, three coffers
whose depth is not known. A fewness
of fine words, a fewness of cows in grass,
a fewness of friends around ale. Truth,
nature, knowledge. Three after-sorrows.
Hush, stop, listen! Three timid brothers.
Three slender things that best support the world.

after Kuno Meyer

ELEGY FOR ANY OCCASION

                    bats   and trees
grief   and boredom   buzzards
and mountains   any permutation
         thereof

         how without you
dying   should these   tokens
         of what   abiding

hope   amount   to more
         than unavailing

splendour   again   a tired old

         sunset   over Leschangie

MEMORY

the cloud of your passing
                    passed close and low
a bird's shadow
                    where no bird flew

DESIRE PATH

Ever so cantily takes off down
the road in his britches and boots except

ford-the-burn   jump-the-stile   hug-the-ditches
James Mitchell Carrier Parcels

& Goods Delivered bearing from
Mrs Letitia Amelia Burnett

to the minister's wife a copy
of Mr Dickens' *Bleak House*

finds his route barred by the A96.
Too late we realize a man may climb

Bennachie but shall no longer
walk from village to town; it cannot

be done. Roadside cats' eyes once
were stars to steer by and before

he gangs agley on Tyrebagger Hill
I had wished him convey to Dr

Timothy Baker of Old Aberdeen
these essays wrapped in wax paper.

Dabs of afternoon smirr blot
the address to chromatography

trace-work; my best broad hand
comes off on the carrier's sleeve

and much that was precious goes
with it. Again I hear the last

stagecoach's horn, and behind
its echo a dreamt delivery from

---

the nineteenth century coming empty-
handed and lovely over the hill.

ALTITUDE MIGRANTS

Laid plateau-wide like a tablecloth the snow and winter is set.

Blin drift, sneepa, owerblaw, skifter, feucher, skirlie, wauff.

Turning white I will keep the red stripe over my eye.

Upended bog cotton paint brushes standing in their dirty brown water.

Pass me going down/coming up on our seasonal funicular circuit.

Sea level falls away like the shingle under a sea-swimmer's feet.

Tonsured heads of far-away hills waking on hay bales of cloud.

Croaking in Gaelic I will not surrender my false Greek p.

Stop-go motion blur of the mink who comes after and predates me.

Playfully towards me the summit lobs the small white ball of a snow
    bunting.

The horn-tack snowshoe effect, the fan-tail spread like a card trick.

White I cannot see the white for the white for the.

Cannot hear the thought of you for your sudden thundering noise.

Black still black the ptarmigan's eye patch coquettishly fluttered
    against the snow.

WHITE NIGHTS

homage to Webern

over
nighttime roofs
to-and-fro

oystercatchers'
circling song
where

white
dusk-dawns converging
fuse-vanish

vanish-fuse
converging dawn-dusks
white

where
song circling
oystercatchers'

fro-and-to
roofs nighttime
over

BENNACHIE RED

'The discovery on Mars of macaulayite—found nowhere on earth but
Bennachie— prompted speculation that the first Aberdonians were
natives of the red planet.'
                    – *Antiquities of Aberdeenshire*

           Thieves' marks carved
        on Bennachie summit blast
this land as snatched from underfoot:
old stone-cutters driven out
        and old crofts seized where rust-
           red cattle calved;

           where under harvest
        moons from Grassic Gibbon's
day blood-red macaulayite
is breach-born from the mountainside.
        Raw the old earth's bones
           and scar-faced

           while ruddy alien
        god you are, Mars—sailed
behind the moon—you circle lost,
deconsecrated, pockmarked host,
        and, blushing, swim in spilt
           communion wine.

BEITHE-LUIS-NIN/BIRCH-ROWAN-ASH

Who invented speech, and when and where did he invent it?

Not hard to relate. It was Fenius Farsaidh at the Tower of Nimrod ten years after its destruction.

The schoolmen asked Fenius to choose for them one of the many languages they had carried from abroad, that speech might not be the gift of all but theirs alone.

Then their language was chosen from the many and named for one of that tribe, Gaelic being named for Gaedil son of Angen son of Whiteknee son of Whitehand son of Greek Agnumon.

What was best and finest of all languages was selected for Gaelic, what was easier and more pleasurable in the saying, and those sounds for which no signs existed in other alphabets were given expression in Ogham; and for every obscure sound in other tongues a place was found in Gaelic owing to its intricacy beyond all speech.

Fenius Farsaidh is the same who discovered these alphabets, namely Hebrew, Greek, Latin and Ogham, and the last of these is the most exact for being discovered last.

Some claim it is not from men that Ogham vowels are named but from trees, namely: chieftain trees, peasant trees, herb trees and shrub trees.

Chieftain trees: oak, hazel, holly, apple, ash, yew, fir;
peasant trees: alder, willow, birch, elm, whitethorn, aspen, mountain-
    ash;
herb trees: furze, heather, broom, bog-myrtle, rushes;
shrub trees: black-thorn, elder, spindle-tree, test-tree, honeysuckle,
    bird-cherry, white-hazel.

Owing to its resemblance to the trunk of that tree, *beithe* is named for the birch and therefore on birch was written the first Ogham inscription, namely: thy wife will be taken from you unless you watch her. Therefore is b the first letter of the Ogham alphabet. And so with the other letters, among them:

a delight to the eye the rowan	*luis*/rowan
colour of a lifeless one	*sail*/willow
an end to peace, spear-shafts made from it; maw of a weaver's beam hewn from it (the weaver's beam is raised in time of peace)	*nin*/ash
a meet of hounds; formidable for its thorns	*huath*/white-thorn
higher than bushes	*duir*/oak
a third of a wheel; one of a chariot wheel's three timbers	*tinne*/holly
fair wood; all consume its nuts	*coll*/hazel
shelter of a wild hind	*queirt*/apple-tree
the most high beauty	*muin*/vine-tree
greener than pastures	*gort*/ivy
a healer's strength	*ngetal*/broom
the hedge of a stream	*straiph*/black-thorn
the red flush of shame	*ruis*/elder

Now all these are wood names found in the Ogham Books of Woods and not come from men.

Five certain numbers: 72 tribes, 72 counsellors with them, 72 tongues sundered among them, 72 scholars along with Fenius to learn the tongues, 72 paces the height of the tower.

Definite is the Greek alphabet, more exact than the Hebrew. Definite the Latin alphabet, more exact than the Greek. But more definite than the Latin the *Beithe-Luis-Nin* of the Ogham, for it was invented last.

What single word comprehends all four divisions of the scholar's primer? Not hard. The word 'alphabet'.

Auraicept na n-Éces/The Scholars' Primer

THE PORCH-LIGHT

Birchwood ankle-deep in leafy mulch:
borrowed green of a buried can of Grolsch,
all living streams iced over or departed;
wrecks of chestnuts echoing, empty-hearted,
hollow victories woodpeckers tap
on trunks picked open for a place to sleep.
The breeze's whistling summons and refines
itself to a buzzard's wheep beyond the pines,
where arrowheads of geese above the farm
lock onto, lose their target, and reform.
Eggbox hills that line the far horizon
draw a ribbon out of slowly-rising
tracks that circle straggling round the village
millponds, quarry, setts, a gateless gate-lodge
keeping nothing in or out. A dipper
breasts the Don and wades in deep and deeper;
a porch-light glimpsed among trees might be my house.
The path wants feet, it will not matter whose.
Whose woods these are I couldn't claim to know,
the way I go all ways, on in back through.

THE QUARRY-POND

The ways we take   are a part of ourselves
but lead   through hazard
the pond is too deep   and needs signs
yet first when   we came here

in the season   of yellow wagtails
walking the bounds   of untouched
possibility and   the fine-veined
evening filtered   through the pines

with what   unconcern
we met   in the woods
the gaze of   its muddy-
bright depths   forced up from

the source   the silverbright
eyes of the granite   submerged
that first time   the blustering
rush of air   from the windfarm

blades behind us   the buzzard nests
and mountain view   so close could
we have seen them   had we
known   they were there

LETTER TO JOSEPH MASSEY

Entirely ordinary   Aberdeenshire   farm buildings
      and how they   behave   undeceived
by heat in   September   shimmering   greeny-blue-
      orange across   loanings   subject
to currents   counter-currents   of breezes   parting
      gamely   the corn rigs   round our waists

farm buildings   open   both ends   that warehouse
      light   the remnants of air   and echoes
we found   an empty cottage   in the woods
      and a milk bottle   still on   the windowsill
out past   the tyre hills   and silage stacks
      where the motorbikes   keep busy

and under their bark   the wing-drift   and song-burst
      of the serious   coming year's turn
announced by way   of rain   that prints   the fields
      in what we are   and then   passing
low   among trees   in his sling   my son
      noiseless   and slick   as an owl

DIP

Lightly depressing
         the pedal I sink
                  the Mither Tap

through the pine-line
         on the near ridge
                  entering

the dip in the road:
         not the usual turn,
                  but serviceable and

leaving us time and to spare
         to throw up a volley
                  of gravel where

we park for a withershins
         circling of the new loch
                  and its lone golden-

eye, his fellows passing
         overhead like a host of
                  balloons he's let go

and flying off over
         our house: there
                  before us,

constellating
         from wingbeat
                  to wingbeat

the changeable—
         that scattered grit
                  a council lorry

flings in our faces
         and the wiper as quickly
                  bats away.

HYPERION DREES HIS WEIRD

eftir Hölderlin

Gracie speerits, ayont
  i' the licht ye wauner on saft yird.
    The gidlie gleetin caller air
      tigs ye doucely lik a lassie's
        haund spielin a jig
          on the Muses' fingerboord.

The guids lik doverin weans
  souch wi' nae forethocht;
    still an on their speerits blume
      lik fauldit flooers, leally keept,
        their haily een keekin oot
          on a gleg month o' muins ta come.

Thaur's nae plaice heiven–
  sent gi'en us ta rist,
    puir doolin fowk forbye
      wha blintly dwine and fa
        frae ane oor ta the neist,
          lik a burn thrawn frae heuch
            ta heuch endweys fer aye and aye.

yird: earth, *gleetin:* shining, *caller air:* breeze, *tigs:* touches, *doucely:* gently, *spielin:* playing, *doverin:* sleepy, *weans:* children, *souch:* breathe, *leally:* carefully, *keekin:* looking, *gleg:* clear, *doolin:* suffering, *forbye:* besides, *dwine:* waste, *heuch:* ledge, *endweys:* ceaselessly

SONNETS TO ROBERT FERGUSSON

1

Fegs, Rab, fa's thon gowk stravaigin
doon the road, clarty locks shakin
and wheemerin o' his spaul-banes achin?
　　　　Puir bummer,
dreein a darg o' tattie-howkin
　　　　aa bluidy summer.
Keekin oot frae Auld Meldrum
ye maun hae seen Bennachie's lum
faur a haill clamjamfrie cam
　　　　fer a stramash
in Roman times, lea'in sum
　　　　puir fowk gey hasht.
But fit's that noo stramash I'm hearin'?
Jouk in here, or we're forfaren!

fegs: truly, *fa's:* who's, *gowk:* fool, *stravaigin:* wandering, *clarty:* dirty,
wheemerin: complaining, *spaul-banes:* back-bones, *bummer:* singer,
dreein: bearing, *darg:* job of work, *tattie-howkin:* potato-picking,
keekin: looking, *maun:* must, *lum:* chimney, *faur:* where, *haill:* whole,
clamjamfric: crowd, *stramash:* fight, *gey hasht:* badly injured, *fit's:* what's,
jouk: duck, *forfaren:* done-for

2

Some het aquavit'll wet yer thrapple,
I dare say. The weither's aafa dreich:
it's chuckin—*dingin* it doon. My Doric
comes and goes: I'm also nae sae supple
wi' the habbie, Rab; hence these sonnets.
Bank that fire up. Pass me a *Sunday Post*
('Vote No to Save the Union'): let it toast,
its hopes sent up in flames, just like the Nats'.
But what is our nation?, well you might ask now
'14's been added to the bingo card
of Scotland's jackpot years the wrong side claimed,
and Bingo caller Cameron tells us how
the loser gets one Devo Max and, coward
dafties that we are, we throw the game.

het: hot, *thrapple:* windpipe, *aafa dreich:* quite dreary, *chuckin:* raining
hard, *habbie:* Habbie stanza, *dafties:* fools

3

Purple and yellow polka-dot town houses
hewn from every kind of rock do not
this city make, that takes its granite neat
and cuts dead all your garish non-grey choices.
That flash of red's a trawler from Stavanger,
or is it a Tennents T glimpsed through the haar?
There's nary a lantern I'll not follow here,
shipmate, if it means us dropping anchor.
Ah Scotland, deck for the bard fit music hall,
ringing with Burns's lays or pibroch's skreed;
but you've not heard of Burns (though he loved you),
the sailors pile into a strip bar while—
remembering your line that 'music's dead'—
a busking piper hangs his head, soaked through.

haar: sea-mist, *pibroch's skreed:* bagpipe music

4

Burns, Rab Burns, makar o' 'Tam o' Shanter'—
thon carle whase statue stands aff Union Street
and whase scunnert, bronze een weel micht greet
like oors for Scotland and the spell she's under.
Westminster warlocks gatherin i' the mirk
gae primpit like the beldams frae Macbeth
and, ech, bite haurd for auld wives wantin teeth—
each uggsome form thrawin off its cutty sark.
The dowie ghaists reek worse than alley cat-spray:
Gordon Broon spoons up his Tory porridge,
Jim Murphy does a turn as Harry Lauder,
Alistair Darling's eyebrows dance the strathspey,
and, what's this, Tony Blair, Bob Geldof, George
Galloway, marching wi' the Orange Order!

makar: poet, *carle:* fellow, *scunnert:* disgusted, *een weel micht greet:* eyes
well might weep, *oors:* ours, *mirk:* dark, *primpit:* bedecked, *beldams:*
witches, *uggsome:* ugly, *cutty sark:* short skirt, *dowie:* dismal

5

But aa Scots sloch aits, scrieved Samy Johnson.
He'll be a lang time ficklin o'er his brose
afore yer haemil leid stairts mouin prose
the like o' whilk the doctor hings his rants on.
Grub Street's 'lexipharian' non-pareil!
Ye didna wiss the Doc tae lear the Scots
mair fantoush, gawsy weys tae dink their thochts,
wi' aye sae mony gleg tongues on the payroll.
There's bings o' Pictish stanes in Auld Brythonic
and Arthur Johnston's Inverurie Latin;
MacDiarmid made his Shetland stanes speak Norn
and Gaelic corrieneuchs are aye a tonic.
But queen o' aa's a tongue mair aften shat on:
this throughother speech, this Scots, in which we're twan.

sloch aits: eat oats, *scrieved:* wrote, *ficklin:* puzzling, *brose:* porridge,
haemil leid: homely tongue, *mouin:* mouthing, *whilk:* which, *hings:*
hangs, *wiss:* need, *lear:* teach, *fantoush:* pretentious/showy, *gleg:* smart,
bings: heaps, *corrieneuchs:* conversations, *twan:* twinned

6

Gies your gab, I might say, though another
Robert (Garioch) pulled this trick first, years back.
I bounce my voice off his and get yours back
as well: the banter of aa loons thegither.
I've couthied up across the decades aince
before, Rab, to a countryman of mine,
James Clarence Mangan—have you met? You maun
exchange verse letters or a sonnet sequence.
But aye loons, loons! The only quine you'll find
in Mangan's Róisín Dubh, and Aberdeen's
a statue-park for chain-mailed beardy blokes.
Where's Mother Scotia, 'that beauty lang had kend'?
Sharp on the breeze, a rowst of high-pitched quines
fades to a silent dark beyond the docks.

gies your gab: talk to me, *aa loons thegither:* all boys together, *couthied:*
cosied, *aince:* once, *maun:* should, *aye:* always, *quine:* girl, *kend:* known,
rowst: rowdiness

7

Ane place ye'll hear a lassie's voice is sangschaws
doon The Blue Lamp: 'There lived twa sisters
in ane bower...'. Songs whaur hairt-wae festers
wi' unfinished business, sair and anxious.
And someone's for the chop: 'He's coorted the eldest
wi' his penknife...' But then she kills the younger
quine for spite, wha'd ne'er done ocht tae wrong her.
Songs that chowk the dulie lungs like coal-dust.
You'd a braw voice for your 'Lassie My Dearie',
but a maiden in song is soon unmade:
the hairt's mair slauchterhoose than nunnery.
Strike up while you can wi' 'Lassie Lie Near Me',
but ballads want blood: 'There's either a maid
or a milk-white swan drooned in the dams of Minorie.'

ane: one, *sangschaws:* song-shows/concerts, *hairt-wae:* heartbreak, *sair:*
sore, *dulie:* sad, *braw:* fine, *hairt:* heart

8

Tumblin doon the howff stairs wi' a curt aith
while airtin for the gents', ye end up arselins
i' the strone and gleeked by some coarse loons.
Auld breeks, auld freend throu daftest days o'poortith,
and duddy trooser-seat: fit times ye hae
brookin yer puir *embarras de richesse*
o' aa the jyle cells, bar stuils, braes an ditches
ye've made yer awn through years o' sons and wae.
Yet part we maun, ye tell yer breeks, then lab
them oot the winda on some hoosemaid's heid.
Who wears the troosers noo? On my heid too,
amang Edina's roses, yer breeks drop,
and braithing deep the fairty guff ye dreed
I ken the midden whaur aa poems grow.

howff: inn, *aith:* oath, *airtin for:* making for, *arselins:* on your backside,
strone: gutter, *gleeked:* mocked, *breeks:* trousers, *daftest:* maddest,
poortith: poverty, *duddy:* ragged, *brookin:* enjoying, *puir:* poor, *awn:*
own, *sons:* plenty, *wae:* woe, *maun:* must, *lab:* throw, *Edina's roses:* full
chamberpots, *guff:* smell, *dreed:* endured

9

Your words to me are 'Caller Water', a *fons
Bandusiae* whose living streams I sup.
Scotland is Greece and Rome: I lap it up,
and dream of lochans thronged with nymphs and fauns.
But these days 'Caller Water' comes in bottles
with Alka Seltzer bubbles for effect,
and nature privatized is nature fucked—
a dying grouse some bastard gillie throttles.
Where wee whaups picked their way on sandy feet
Donald Trump lines up a hole-in-one
and buzzing choppers fill the air, not lav'rocks.
Lose 'Caller Water', choose black gold: reboot
as Scotland's corporate Anacreon,
laureate of share quotes, Mercs and oil rigs.

whaups: curlews, *lav'rocks:* larks

10

This traipsin's takin affa lang to get
you saufly hame frae Aberdeen tae Embra.
Becalmed in this vagabond penumbra
in your brouky claes and buits ye tug at—
a Donside Rimbaud—fit ye need's a hobby.
Have you tried creative writing? 'Unlock
Your Inner Poet', 'Self-Publish Your First Book'—
ye ken the drill—'Connecting With the Habbie.'
I'd sign you up, but some young poet you are:
nae website, nae on Twitter, New Gen reject—
ye're gangin naewey fest. It matters, son;
your retro *maudit* act's fair fooshtit-dour.
I'll do PR, you get your poems rejigged.
We relaunch with: 'The New Don Paterson'.

saufly hame: safely home, *brouky claes:* dirty clothes, *buits:* boots, *fit:* what, *gangin naewey:* going nowhere, *fooshtit-dour:* quite stale

11

Fornenst Dunnottar Castle, history's
a teemit skull, spugs an foumaws threidin
its een like weyrs to stap the sicht they're dreidin
o' yet mair Covenanters, Whigs and Tories.
Lang syne, here sic an sic dang sae an sae:
here hunders birned and stairved and drouned in keech
as God ordained and ministers would preach;
nou as then the ootleuk's gey wanchancy.
Gin the stanes could speak they'd airt yer glower
to whaur Bill Wallace stuid and bid ye ken
the foumaw's nest they mynd aince on thon swaird,
fer history's the glamour and the glaur
o' ages caldrife tae the works o' men—
a butterfly perked on the Bruce's swuird.

fornenst: alongside, *teemit:* empty, *spugs:* sparrows, *foumaws:* fulmars,
weyrs: needles, *sic an sic:* such and such, *dang:* smote, *sae an sae:* so and
so, *keech:* shit, *ootleuk:* outlook, *gey wanchancy:* very ill-omened, *gin:* if,
airt yer glower: direct your gaze, *mynd:* remember, *aince:* once, *swaird:*
sward, *glamour:* enchantment, *glaur:* dirt, *caldrife:* indifferent, *perked:*
perched, *swuird:* sword

12

A butterfly flees aboon Union Street,
where wage slaves, in your day gart to scriven,
dunt at keyboards, data-input-driven.
I follow your words, but all I do's repeat,
repeat, repeat, just like your scratchy quill.
Deposition, divorce and testament—
like art without the rhyme-words at the end—
pile up, words no one reads and no one will.
You write your testament and date it blank.
It's only a convention, after all,
a canty farewell practised like a lesson.
Death, like scrivening, comes down to ink:
a paper signed, you handing me your will
across the desk to copy and pass on.

flees aboon: flies above, *gart:* made, *dunt:* strike, *canty:* playful

13

'In the cells': your final tumble ends
not on a stairwell but a Bedlam ward,
whaur manin bare-scud doiterels gae afeart
o' rattons like a plague their last duim sends.
Ane puir quaichin bedlar's Jesus Christ,
anither's Charlie Stewart hissel retoured:
twa keengs o'keengs doverin i' the clart
an keepin up their dirdum till aa's wheesht.
Throu yer snell deid-thraw and fit comes efter
I hear nae cruinin frae the ghaistly choir,
but aye the river o' Scots song flowen away
and spierin doucely as it gaes if there
isna time fer—gie it laldy—ane mair
chorus o' 'The Birks of Invermay'.

manin: moaning, *bare-scud:* naked insane, *afeart:* afraid, *rattons:* rats,
duim: doom, *quaichin bedlar:* screaming inmate, *Charlie Stewart hissel
retoured:* Bonnie Prince Charlie himself come back, *keengs:* kings,
doverin: dozing, *clart:* dirt, *dirdum:* racket, *wheesht:* silent, *snell deid-
thraw:* harsh death-rattle, *cruinin:* mourning, *spierin doucely:* asking
softly, *gie it laldy:* perform with brio

14

Yet part we maun, wi' teemit wame,
nae gweed braid claith tae aither's name
an nae mair crack as ye tramp hame,
         forwandert chiel
wi' naewey 'neath the mune's bricht leam
         tae gie ye biel.
Ettlin tae souch fareweel I'm drooned
oot by the traffeck soothwart-boond,
an Aberdein is dreich, dreich grund
         fer a gaun-aboot
wha tholes tho he can scantlins staund
         ilk bygaein plowt,
an hailsed by nae lumb's cadgy reek
alane throu wund and mirk maun treik.

teemit wame: empty belly, *gweed braid claith:* good broad cloth, *aither's:* either's, *crack:* dialogue, *forwandert chiel:* lost child, *naewey:* nowhere, *leam:* glow, *biel:* shelter, *ettlin tae souch:* trying to sigh, *soothwart-boond:* south-bound, *gaun-aboot:* wanderer, *tholes:* endures, *scantlins staund:* hardly stand, *ilk bygaein plowt:* each passing shower, *hailsed:* welcomed, *lumb's cadgy reek:* chimney's friendly smoke, *alane:* alone, *wund and mirk:* wind and dark, *treik:* tramp

THE KING O'ER THE WATER

Mariolatrous Northlands: echoes
along choir-stalls of Dunbar's
salutation to Margaret Tudor;
the Spanish envoy's horse
spied through dirty snowflakes
at the head of the valley by
the milk-maid's son, his round
face at a trellis window against
the roughcast harling.

Here the counter-reformation
shall be a matter of light thick
as a coach-house window:
early-morning shadows fringing
the Virgin's dress on the chapel
wall, a shade of azure un-
dreamt of south of the Dee.

The structure we see today may
conceal an earlier structure
now invisible. Uneven flag-
stones pitch you dreamily into
the future anterior: 'The ninth
Earl will be charged with treason...'
The word 'caducity', a falling
away: paused on, underlined
in a letter pressed by a French
spy into your hands.

In fifteen sixty-two Mary
Queen of Scots sleeps diagonally
in this chamber, triangulating
old alliances, old betrayals.
The scarlet tips of her hair
have been scratched by the artist
from oak-bark, a cochineal harvest
staining the hands like berries,
the perfect hellish red tinging

the human-headed beasts
that drift across the painted ceiling.

'Bankrupted after the Rising,
the family will be forced
to sell the estate...' To snatch
from the air a living tradition
and return it thence, the slow
going-down of aura behind
the Torridon Hills in the west,
a gift-shop attendant
clutching the chip-and-pin
machine aloft in search of a signal.

Late suns tickle the cinquefoil,
the fingers of moss round
the architrave, and a too-tempting
sentence beginning 'History is...'
formulates itself on the library
desk that overlooks the herb
garden. We reach for a predicate
as the turn-pike stair reaches,
twist after twist, for the priest-
hole and its skeleton bricked
into the wall—

we reach but the sentence
will stay unfinished, the music
mistress come suddenly
into the room singing
of the shattered-crystal beauty
of lost causes, their secret
laughter and unremembered
vindication in the eyes
of our King o'er the water.

                    Delgatie Castle

TO GAVIN DOUGLAS, TRANSLATOR, BY THE DON

Amang dirk skuggis standand full drery. – Eneados

As I cam in by Monymusk   of the red eaves,
and doon by Alford's dale   its windy blasts
and ventosities   *the moon was shinin clear*
on me a seeker after preferment and a deanship
who foundered under the Greek Ys of a flight
of passing cranes and unearthed the first nature poems
among dark shadows where English lies pooled
in Scots, Latin and Gaelic. Let me hook you,
Mantuan, into English with the crook of a yogh—
₃—my sly alien letter future scribes will strike
from the text. Mooring on your shores I coax
a fire from kindling brought by the swineherd
and leave for Venus the bones of a coney
scraped from the skillet. I ponder the oak-knots
on my lectern, that swim before my eyes
like the Stygian tide scumbled by Charon's oars;
I enter that whirlpool and am there, sooner
than the quill can puncture the ice-dermis
of the inkstand. Presences loom among
dark shadows drearily recalled for my embrace:
do you spurn me Dido, my fingers running over
your absent face? I make out your faint *Remember me*,
sad empty cry of unappeased complaint,
and my ears teem with a chaos of echoes
hung in the air, a glamourie of one world
coating another. Where we alchemize whisky
from the Don, a tongued-at dream of translation
panned from its gravel beds, its shed skin too
hangs in the air and intoxicates the leaves
of madder and dog rose. Come evening the wind
blusters and the Sibyl's leaves dispel like leaves,
a frustration of words folded back into themselves,
unheard and unheeded, where thoughts against
thoughts catch and draw blood. Returning from
the underworld, I find the realm of light
used up; squander myself in the small failures
of ambition and advancement until I too

darken, struck with plague, and my face retreats
from the candle's halo into final shadow.

1496

THE HOOPS

An attempted father-in-law

1

But tell me, how did you
die most often: lost

at sea, in a train crash?
Accounts and even

your name would vary
from year to year until

what with tale upon tale
of you spun by one

with only your staying
lost at heart

it must have seemed
the reasonable thing

to resort—no, really—
to a death of your own.

2

Hysterical use of
the second-person:

it's just a convention;
an elegy is a poem

involving an absence
drawn from life.

Reliquary of
guessed-at gestures

and a stage-set
of 70s Wishaw

assembled in the dark—
a milk bottle top's

curled lip
moustachioed with ice

where the boots pass
in the morning,

the scoured doorstep
sunk at its centre

like a pillow
and soft enough

for the wee dog
unwoken by

your tread.

3

The absent take
up so much more

space than the quick
selfishly expand

to fill any available
void we'd been

keeping for you
footballer   soldier

shop steward
this train of thought

divides over three
countries in Glasgow

Belfast   Burnley
a beau on a bike

ducked down a side-
street   a Scotsman

at large with
a demobbed

squaddie's bravado:
Erin go Bragh

on the karaoke
machine if you

fancy a sing-
along and *A don't*

give a damn
tae whit place

ye belang.

4

A peewit over
Belfast Lough

tunes and untunes
a gibbering walkie–

talkie but who
is copying who

a patrol's headlights
return a cat's eye–

lasers and in that
moment become

the hunted while
the peewit cries

tewit-weet-
weet-tew

5

Curious as to your
genetic make-up

skin tone freckles
and other small habits

propensity to whistle
or hum but lacking

a primary witness
we have explored

other avenues
and call in evidence

(we will know you
when we see him)

one as yet
in a warm darkness

whose line in
mimickry of you

is billed to astound.

6

All through the game I
see you now playing

at Parkhead
feet would be stamping

there would be no
hearing your own

name on the pitch
where you ran

for the one free space
ahead and rose for

the ball as though
jumping through hoops

i.m. Robert Canavan

TIDES

1

A wagtail's tail measuring grain
by grain salt to judge from its St
Vitus' dance seesawing over
the driveway and on down the hill
to the park fitful yet careful
completing one circuit of the
estate and starting another
it keeps on from morning till night

2

as to the dawn-numb body the
circulatory system these
slip-roads to the A96
the dark car dashboard fruit-machines
to life and the wakeful fireflies
of drive-time wink each to the next
until cresting the hill we find
unwrapped by first light tower-blocks

3

part of an oilrig a giant's
yo-yo on the roundabout by
the turn for the airport traffic
sluggish today as the price of
a barrel of North Sea crude the
talk of little else for offshore
workers lighting up anent the
terminal before flying out

4

girders cabins portaloos pipes
exoskeletons of venture
capital in the unfinished
business park seek tax breaks 'Invest'
screams Alec Ferguson red-faced
from a billboard quick flows the Don
and deep lies the coastal shelf of
waiting untapped revenue streams

5

implacable Petropolis
where from the car window should I
seek your softer edges rabbits
grazing on the traffic islands
a deer at the edge of the woods
still uncleared for the new estates
snout cocked by the electric fence
pulsing in time to its heartbeat

6

lit like Orthodox shrines the rigs
of passing HGVs honour
a god whose ichor runs black god
whose heavy-breathing burn-off flares
like St Elmo's fire in the night
out where the Piper Alpha slick
washed and refluxed round dead seabirds
all summer before breaking up

7

astray on the outer suburbs'
works floor of greenbelt-destruction
faceless strolls a schoolboy past the
sandpit of balletic diggers
and forklifts and compels amid
their bustle my gaze sole smudge on
the move not screaming hi-vis lime
but bleak and sorry human grey

8

and pulling into the drive past
the brash children skateboarding down
the hill how not be pleased with the
dull day after day of it who
stand shaking out salt and soy sauce
over the frying pan framed as
though lost in the kitchen window
against the evening's slow black tide

The Reed Bunting Unseen

A Camouflage Garden
For Ian Hamilton Finlay

'J'ai cru à des responses de la pierre.' – Guillevic

LITTLE SPARTA/SPANDAU

Arriving in Britain from the Bahamas in the 1940s, the young Ian Hamilton Finlay was disoriented by the wartime absence for security reasons of road-signs. Making his way to Oxford, where he hoped to stay with Sidney Keyes, he was mistaken for a German parachutist, an episode from which he extricated himself only with some difficulty. Contemporaneously a genuine parachutist, Rudolf Hess, was dropping into Scotland on unspecified business. It has been suggested that Hess hoped to meet Ian Hamilton—not to be confused with the Scot's near-namesake, let alone the younger English poet of the same name—considered to be the most Germanophile member of Churchill's cabinet, to hammer out who knows what dastardly alternative Molotov-Ribbentrop pact. If so, his capture meant the trip came to nothing more than a dress rehearsal for Hess's long post-war years of confinement in Spandau. Later in life Ian Hamilton Finlay would dream of recreating the garden created in prison by Hess's brother in arms, Albert Speer. Finlay's fascination with SS paraphernalia has discomfited many, but while the martial fantasies that fuel his work represent one obvious source, Finlay's agoraphobia may have played its part too, confining him as it did to his Stonypath home for thirty years. (Speer, meanwhile, dealt with his own confinement by 'walking' round the world in the exercise yard at Spandau, using guidebooks and maps to chart his route from country to country, proceeding eastwards through Asia and Siberia before crossing the Bering Strait and ending his 'journey' in Mexico.) To one unable to cross the street to insult his enemies, the leap from an angry letter to the Arts Council to Blitzkrieg of the imagination, if one might so characterise Finlay's flyting campaigns, is short and seductive. A garden is not a retreat, Finlay insisted, it is an attack. Equally, if tirade upon tirade is what one's audience deserves, why not swing to the other extreme and give them, on one level at least, precisely nothing (concrete poetry is a *silent* poetry, Finlay insisted, for all that MacDiarmid associated Finlay with the noisy 'happenings' of Alexander Trocchi and other 'cosmopolitan scum' of the 1960s). Rarely can a silence have been as broodingly aggressive as Finlay's.

To return to Rudolph Hess: as a student I met an American whose father had been the German's prison doctor in Spandau. Hess lost a rib in the First World War, he told me, but the man in Spandau was in possession of the full set. Here was a classic urban myth, the stand-in/fall-guy content to serve out long decades in prison while the true Hess luxuriated in *Odessa File* exile in Paraguay or Brazil. Had he ventured beyond the bounds of Little Sparta, who knows what mischief Ian Hamilton Finlay might have got up to. Instead, he made of himself an ecstatic prisoner of the imagination. But to paraphrase Jean Genet, better to become *un captif amoureux* than set a thousand prisoners free. Who has been freer than Finlay, between his impotent, house-bound rage, and its accompanying world-conjuring, world-dismissing imaginative *fiat?* *Il faut cultiver son jardin? Il faut cultiver sa prison.*

FIRST CONTACT

'In the event of unforeseen parachute release, proceed with extreme caution. Remember your training. Establish and confirm your exact location as far as possible. Remove all identifying insignia from clothing, destroy all incriminating documents, and avoid unnecessary civilian contact. If in a group and challenged by parties unknown, allow your superior or the most confident member of your company (French- or German-speaking) to speak on your behalf. If suspicion is not aroused on first contact and subsequently, do not become over-familiar with locals. Your position will remain at all times precarious. Expression of political opinions is strongly discouraged. If in need of shelter or a hiding place, outbuildings and gardens are especially recommended.'
(*Parachute Operations: Training and Preparedness*, RAF, 1940)

CREATION MYTH

One letter leads
to another and
there is a name.

Not to be left
out the place
comes along too.

GARDEN FEATURE, LITTLE SPARTA

Le stile, *c'est l'homme même.*

A CLEARANCE

Sun to morning dew: 'Get off my land.'

A CAMOUFLAGE GARDEN

R D B TING

EE UN N S

UNSEEN

REED BUNTING

IT'S WAR

Man against man.
Man against sheep.
Sheep against man.
Sheep against grass.
Sheep against sheep.
Mountain against sky.
Grass against mountain.
Sheep against sky.
Sky against nothing.

YOUR SHEEP, MY SHEEP

blue arse, red arse

DEAD SHEEP

dǝǝɥs pɐǝp

TEXT POEM

cannot be sent (no coverage)

CULTURAL MATERIALISM

To recreate outline
of peaks against horizon
trace pencil over
top of these letters.

SUNDIAL IN RAIN

needs winding

ECLOGUE

Daphne is turned to a laurel.
Apollo too turns to a laurel.
They live side by side.

DICHTUNG = CONDENSARE

Considered in geological time the highest peaks are the youngest, mere seismological upstarts, and the most venerable your unremarkable braes and hillocks, worn down by untold ages. Mountaineering's final threshold may therefore be less the unclimbed routes of the Himalayas but flat earth, and the truest Mount Parnassus somewhere at sea level. Mindful of this and in best *Monty Python*-style I hold fast to each lamp post, fearful of sliding horizontally away to my doom. In the same way the final frontier for poetic epic, as much as for lyric, may lie not in expansion but contraction, in whole worlds of noisy expression condensed into silence or the next best thing, Finlayesque one-word poems trembling on its edge. I think of Tim Robinson's sublime meditations on walking the cliff edges of Aran and Connemara, and dream of the final step across that verbal threshold, implied but not taken; the metrical foot raised and about to come down on the emptiness over its brink—

ROBESPIERRE, WEEDING

Off with their heads!

APOLLON TÉRRORISTE

A Greek male has been detained under
the Incitement to Artistic Hatred Act.

GEOLOGY AS SMALLTALK

pebble chattered to sand

GROTTO

Fit offering for
a god, the clouds in the pool,
a beaker of sky.

A BOUQUET FOR THOMAS EDMONSTON

the dwarf willow
sprig pressed into
its page in the guide

ON NOT BEING SEEN

'I didn't see you at camouflage training
this morning, Finlay.' 'Thank you, sir.'

(after Frank Carson)

RUINED BUILDINGS/RUINED STONES

Noting an allusion to Poussin in his book on Finlay, *Nature Over Again*, John Dixon Hunt suggests that in the digital era some manner of mobile phone app might enhance the stroller's enjoyment of the garden at Little Sparta. His follow-up comment on the poor phone coverage in the area suggests an instinctive resistance to such an innovation. As mentioned, there were no road-signs in wartime Britain, and in Little Sparta too there are no signs. Its exhibits must speak (or not speak) for themselves. Nor has its history since Finlay's death seen it appropriated by subsequent poets or turned into a Scottish Arvon centre. Who are its ideal inheritors? The world is full of ruined buildings but there are no ruined stones, Finlay's ally/antagonist MacDiarmid observed in 'On a Raised Beach', but it did not take posterity to supply Finlay with ruins, its designer having taken the precaution of smashing its columns in advance. 'The world has been empty since the Romans', after all, as Little Sparta demonstrated more comprehensively the fuller it became. How best should posterity add to the garden and honour its self-cancelling logic at the same time? Abandonment would not be an unFinlayesque destiny for his creation. MacDiarmid's memory might best be honoured, Norman MacCaig suggested, by a two-minute national 'pandemonium', but perhaps what Finlay's needs is a strategic assault on any premature canonisation, which is to say neutering of its legacy, a fresh Battle of Little Sparta to vindicate and if necessary produce the condition of ruin and emptiness against which the garden's glory comes most truly into its own. No medium is more violent than marble, no branch of architecture more violent than funeral masonry. Against such a backdrop the menace of Finlay's battleships and tanks seems oddly softened, these engines of death become so many playthings spilled from the toy box of a capricious Greek god, the giant word-blocks spelling 'THE PRESENT ORDER IS THE DISORDER OF THE FUTURE' illustrating and undoing their message where they lie.

RED-THROATED DIVER, DUMFRIES

Solway *cou coupé*

A GANNET

SOUL/AIR
SOILLEIR
SOLAR
SAILOR
SÙLAIRE

AN AVIARY FOR ALASDAIR MACGILLEMHÌCHEIL

THE LITTLE SORROWING ONE
THE STRONG STOUT BIRD WITH THE SPOT
THE BOG HUNCHBACK
THE MARSH HUNCHBACK
THE FUSSY BODY OF THE STRAND
THE YELLOW ONE OF THE DUNG
THE TRUE BIRD, THE BIRD PAR EXCELLENCE

ONE ANIMAL MAY CONCEAL ANOTHER

dotterel

SIGHTING

A ? is standing on my
copy of *Birds of Scotland.*

SCONSER TRILOGY

i

GATE – POST

ii
buzzard
GATE – POST

iii

GATE – POST

PRE-SOCRATIC NOTES: *HAMILTON ADVERTISER*

Otters' outrage
at one−time−only
enterable rivers.

*

'Way−up−is−way−down'
hillwalkers' Compass
complaints Rise/Fall.

*

Heraclitus (Independent,
Stonypath), denounces
'empty promises'
of 'Know Yourself' Party,
'pledges increased flux'.

A CLEARANCE

An island towed out to sea and sunk.

TRIDENT

Trawlers will occasionally snare
underwater islands in their nets.

BEYOND THESE WALLS

Gardening is silent poetry.
Everything else is open mic.

IRELAND/SCOTLAND: TO THE SÍNEADH/SÌNEADH FADA

Over here we drive on this side of the vowel.

AN ISLAND WEDDING

The bride in her dress
feeding the hens
before bed.

WALLACE STEVENS ON NORTH UIST

Le Monach Isle de Mon Oncle.

SOLUS

SOL   *SOLIS*

SOLAS

SOUL   **SOULLESS**

SOLACE

Solas, North Uist

SÙIL AIR HIORT/ST KILDA VIEW POINT

	siar	iar	iar	iar	iar
	siar	iar	iar	iar	iar
	siar	iar	iar	iar	iar
	siar	iar	iar	iar	iar
	siar	iar	iar	iar	iar
	siar	iar	iar	iar	iar
	siar	iar	iar	iar	iar
	sssssssiar	iar	iar	iar	iar
	ssssssssssssssiar	iar	iar	iar	iar
sssssssssssssssssssssssssssssssssiar	iar	iar	iar	iar	iar

CLOCKWISE ROUND THE ISLAND

DIESEL/DEISEAL

IRON AGE, SIGNIFICANCE UNKNOWN

Ogham incisions read:
'Iron Age, Significance Unknown'

SITE-SPECIFIC

This poem is on permanent loan
to its original location.

SUN ON BLACK CUILLINS

Blue Mordor

LOCUS = LOGOS

'Sràidbhaile An Teanga/Village of Tongue'

ALL IS LITHOGENESIS

O, it is gainless hell.

VILLAGE OF ECHT

Accept no substitutes.

HUT OF SHADOWS CAMERA OBSCURA, LOCHMADDY

rocks and bay
stone-age cinema
the unbroken shot
forever exposed and
not for developing

SCHOOL OF ELOQUENCE

Demosthenes cures himself of his stammer with a mouthful of pebbles.

Dreaming of fresh audiences for its unsuspected eloquence, the tide rolls a mouthful of pebbles on its tongue and spits them out.

The sea takes its words and shoves them back down its throat.

A penitent Demosthenes fills his mouth with pebbles and his stammer is reborn.

THE HERRING GULL SCHOOL

Abstract Expressionist
bombs away
load of old pollocks

HRAUN, DUSS, RØNIS, QUEEDARAUNS, KOLLYARUN

The role of objects is to restore silence, said Beckett. Silent though they are, the stones of Little Sparta possess not just a violent but an explosive force. 'Children pile up PEBBLES as pin-less hand grenades', Finlay writes, but the gate-post grenades in Little Sparta conspicuously retain their pins. The silence of the inanimate does not preclude noisy opinionation, however, if not on the part of the stones then on their behalf. 'It is no compliment to PEBBLES to say, as a modern poet has said of stones, that we can discover no ruined ones', Finlay writes side-swipingly of MacDiarmid's 'On a Raised Beach'. MacDiarmid makes for a very different poetic palaeontologist from Finlay, and if he is keen to stress the absence of 'ruined' stones in his landscape one possible reason is a peculiar silence of his own in that flintiest of poems. To return to geology: humanity is fleeting but the stones are eternal, he insists. They 'came so far out of the water and halted forever', they 'cannot be lured an inch farther / Either on this side of eternity or the other.' They can and have been lured not just an inch, but several miles up and down, as continents collide in cataclysms dwarfing anything the genus *homo sapiens* has inflicted on the planet. Why would MacDiarmid ignore this most obvious of facts? An attempt to address them in Norn ('hraun, duss, rønis, queedarauns, kollyarun') puts some distance between the stones and the Johnny-come-lately formulations of Modern English, but from a stone's point of view, to anthropomorphise for a moment, the differences in time-scale here may be moot. But we are not just anthropomorphising for a moment: 'On a Raised Beach' could hardly be more anthropomorphic about its inhumanism or noisier about the silence that it preaches. The poet picks up a stone and it is 'My own self' he holds, 'The humanity no culture has reached'. But at this point we may be dealing less with a failing of MacDiarmid's than of language itself, and its ability to turn off the author long enough to articulate the inhuman that lies beneath. The tongues are many in which silence seeks relief from the deafening noise it must make on a Shetland beach, and if MacDiarmid's stones need to shout louder about their inhumanity than Finlay's, so be it. Even someone as lacking in the pandemonium factor as the great Francis Ponge is not exempt. He will say no more about the pebble, he announces at the end of his prose poem *'Le galet'*; the disappearance from the pebble's surface of all geological traces as it erodes into sand *'me donne à réfléchir sur les défauts d'un style qui appuie trop sur les mots.'* I lean on the performative contradiction here, and grind Ponge's pebble down slowly into friable sand. But away with this trifling opposition of human and inhuman. 'The place of the PEBBLE in modern aesthetics is that of Natural Man in the philosophy of J.-J. Rousseau', wrote Finlay. What matter who speaks, poet or pebble. I feel the shifting sands under my words, MacDiarmid's stony eternity running out with the low tide.

HARBOUR VIEW TERRACE: HOMAGE TO CALMAC

*gable*ERR*gable*

LIGHT OF EVENING

and the schoolchildren
home off the ferry
and the views out over

the cliffs turned
off for the night
and the tuning-fork

of the sail-boat's
mast striking
the one true note

EILEAN

A lochan, a flat stone
placed at its centre—
Scotland, I have
added an island
to your store.

MERCHANT SHIP ROUTING

wreck

SUBMARINE TRAINING

wreck

LADEN TANKERS

MAGNETIC ANOMALY

wreck

FIRING PRACTICE AREA

RADIO REPORTING

INCOMPLETE SURVEYS

wreck

wreck

Y

ACKNOWLEDGMENTS

The poet is grateful to the following publications where some of these poems have been previously published:

Archipelago, The Burning Bush Revival, Cambridge Literary Review, Causeway/ Cabhsair, Edinburgh Review, Flowering Skullcap (Wurm Press), *The Irish Times, New Walk, Poetry London, The Poetry Review, The Reed Bunting Unseen: A Camouflage Garden for Ian Hamilton Finlay* (Wild Honey Press), *Cincinnati Review, The Same Review, The Yellow Nib, Times Literary Supplement, Spectator, Irish Examiner, The SHOp, Watching My Hands at Work: A Festschrift for Adrian Frazier* (Salmon Publishing), *Peter Fallon: Poet, Publisher, Editor and Translator* (Irish Academic Press), *The Weary Blues, Ash, The Shack: Irish Poets in the Foothills and Mountains of the Blue Ridge* (Wake Forest University Press), *Poetry* (Chicago), *Postcards from Hull* (Hull County Council), *Sketches, Dispatches, Hull Tales and Ballads* (Hull City Council), *Under Travelling Skies: Departures from Larkin* (Hull City Council), *Wales Arts Review, Penguin Book of Irish Poetry* (Penguin).